Becoming a Successful Early Career Researcher

Not that long ago there were fairly clear divisions between researchers at different stages throughout their career, starting with doctoral students then progressing to postdoctoral workers and finishing with academic staff. However, more recently the term Early Career Researcher (ECR) has been introduced partly as a response to their growing importance which has been reflected by their increased respect and status shown by national, international and funding bodies. There are several common features of an ECR's job including the need to establish a professional identity and develop into an independent researcher, competing for grants and increasing one's output of research publications; this book offers proven practical advice to help ECRs kick-start a successful academic career.

With advice on:

- Choosing research topics
- Making best use of a Research Supervisor/Mentor
- Developing your research writing
- Getting published: journals and books
- Writing a research grant/fellowship
- Becoming a supervisor
- Becoming a teacher, and
- Developing your career

This guide will help academics at the start of their career no matter what discipline they are engaged in . . . Arts, Humanities, Sciences or Social Sciences. For example, in sciences and engineering, ECRs are commonly part of a large research team and often have to work in collaborative groups, which requires strong interpersonal skills but can lead to tension in the interaction with one's supervisor or mentor. In contrast, in the arts and humanities and perhaps the social sciences, an ECR is more likely to be an independent scholar with a requirement to work alone, leading to a different type of relationship (but not necessarily any less stressful) with one's supervisor or mentor.

Using case studies from across the subject areas to illustrate key points and give suitable examples this vital guide will help all early career academics.

Adrian Richard Eley, now retired, is a former Senior Lecturer in Medical Microbiology at the University of Sheffield Medical School, UK, and a former Professor of Bacteriology at the United Arab Emirates University, UAE.

Jerry Wellington is Professor and Head of Research Degrees in the School of Education at the University of Sheffield, UK.

Stephanie Pitts is Reader in Music in the Faculty of Arts and Humanities at the University of Sheffield, UK.

Catherine Biggs is Professor of Environmental Engineering in the Faculty of Engineering at the University of Sheffield, UK.

Becoming a Successful Early Career Researcher

Adrian Eley, Jerry Wellington, Stephanie Pitts, and Catherine Biggs

 Routledge
Taylor & Francis Group

LONDON AND NEW YORK

First published 2012
by Routledge
2 Park Square, Milton Park, Abingdon, Oxon OX14 4RN

Simultaneously published in the USA and Canada
by Routledge
711 Third Avenue, New York, NY 10017

Routledge is an imprint of the Taylor & Francis Group, an informa business

British Library Cataloguing in Publication Data
A catalogue record for this book is available from the British Library

Library of Congress Cataloging in Publication Data
Becoming a successful early career researcher/Adrian Eley . . .
[et al.]. p. cm. ISBN 978–0–415–67248–1 (hardback)—
ISBN 978–0–415–67247–4 (paperback)—ISBN 978–0–203–11307–3
(e-book) 1. Universities and colleges—Research. 2. Research—
Vocational guidance. 3. College teachers—Vocational guidance. I. Eley,
Adrian R. II. Title.
  LB2326.3.B43 2012
  378.0072—dc23

                                                    2011051375

ISBN: 978–0–415–67248–1 (hbk)
ISBN: 978–0–415–67247–4 (pbk)
ISBN: 978–0–203–11307–3 (ebk)

Typeset in Galliard
by RefineCatch Limited, Bungay, Suffolk

MIX
Paper from
responsible sources
FSC
www.fsc.org   FSC® C004839

Printed and bound in Great Britain by
TJ International Ltd, Padstow, Cornwall

Adrian wishes to dedicate this book to his father, Derek Eley, for being a constant source of inspiration

Contents

Figures and tables

Figures

Tables

Acronyms and abbreviations

AGCAS	Association of Graduate Careers Advisory Services
AHRC	Arts and Humanities Research Council
BBSRC	Biotechnological and Biological Sciences Research Council
CiLT	Certificate in Learning and Teaching
Co-I	Co-Investigator
COMPETES	Creating Opportunities to Meaningfully Promote Excellence in Technology, Education and Science
CPD	Continuing Professional Development
CPM	Critical Path Method
CV	Curriculum Vitae
CVCP	Committee of Vice-Chancellors and Principals
DA	Diagnostic Assessment
DT	Diagnostic Teaching
ECI	Early Career Investigator
EPSRC	Engineering and Physical Sciences Research Council
ESI	Early Stage Investigator
ESR	Early Stage Researcher
ESRC	Economic and Social Research Council
EU	European Union
EURODOC	The European Council of Doctoral Candidates and Junior Researchers
FTSE	Financial Times (London) Stock Exchange
HE	Higher Education
HEI	Higher Education Institution
HoD	Head of Department
IP	Intellectual Property
MBTI	Myers–Briggs Type Indicator
MRC	Medical Research Council
NERC	National Environment Research Council
NIH	National Institutes of Health
NPA	National Postdoctoral Association
NREC	National Research Ethics Committee

NSF	National Science Foundation
PE	Physical Education
PERT	Programme (or Project) Evaluation and Review Technique
PI	Principal Investigator
QAA	Quality Assurance Agency
RAE	Research Assessment Exercise
RCUK	Research Councils UK
RDF	Researcher Development Framework
REC	Research Ethics Committee
REF	Research Excellence Framework
SRDS	Staff Review and Development Scheme
SURE	Sheffield Undergraduate Research Experience
UCU	University and College Union
UKCGE	UK Council for Graduate Education
UKRSA	UK Research Staff Association

Podcasts

The following podcasts are referred to within this book, and have been identified by 🎙️ followed by the relevant number. All of these podcasts can be accessed on www.routledge.com/books/details/9780415672474

Chapter 1

1. The development of a local postdoc society

A discussion between Dr Kay Guccione, Postdoctoral Researcher Training and Development Advisor, Faculty of Medicine, Dentistry and Health, University of Sheffield and Dr Rachael Elder, Lecturer in the Department of Chemical and Biological Engineering, University of Sheffield.

2. The role of the United Kingdom Research Staff Association (UKRSA)

A discussion between Dr Adrian Eley, Senior Lecturer in the Department of Infection and Immunity, University of Sheffield and Dr Rhiannon Pursall, Postdoctoral Research Associate, School of Biosciences, University of Birmingham.

Chapter 4

3. Writing and getting published

A discussion between Professor Jerry Wellington, Professor in the School of Education, University of Sheffield and Dr Stephanie Pitts, Reader in Music, University of Sheffield.

4. Writing and getting published

A discussion between Professor Jerry Wellington, Professor in the School of Education, University of Sheffield and Dr Simon Keegan-Phipps, Teaching Fellow, Department of Music, University of Sheffield.

Chapter 5

5. Writing and getting published

A discussion between Professor Jerry Wellington, Professor in the School of Education, University of Sheffield and Dr Sara Whiteley, Research Assistant, School of English, University of Sheffield.

Chapter 6

6. Applying for research funding

A discussion between Dr Adrian Eley, Senior Lecturer in the Department of Infection and Immunity, University of Sheffield and Professor Catherine Biggs, Professor in the Department of Chemical and Biological Engineering, University of Sheffield.

7. Applying for research funding

A discussion between Dr Adrian Eley, Senior Lecturer in the Department of Infection and Immunity, University of Sheffield and Dr Steve Mounce, Research Fellow in the Department of Civil and Structural Engineering, University of Sheffield.

Chapter 7

8. Becoming a supervisor

A discussion between Dr Adrian Eley, Senior Lecturer in the Department of Infection and Immunity, University of Sheffield and Dr Michael Trikic, Postdoctoral Researcher, University of Sheffield Medical School.

9. Becoming a supervisor

A discussion between Dr Adrian Eley, Senior Lecturer in the Department of Infection and Immunity, University of Sheffield and Dr Heather Mortiboys, Postdoctoral Researcher, University of Sheffield Medical School.

Chapter 8

10. Becoming a teacher

A discussion between Dr Jon Scaife, Lecturer in the School of Education, University of Sheffield and Mrs Grace Hoskins, PGCE Tutor in the School of Education, University of Sheffield.

11. *Becoming a teacher*

A discussion between Dr Stephanie Pitts, Reader in Music, University of Sheffield and Mr George Parsons, PhD student in the Department of Music, University of Sheffield.

12. *Becoming a teacher*

A discussion between Dr Stephanie Pitts, Reader in Music, University of Sheffield and Dr Luke Desforges, Team Leader in Professional Learning and Teaching Services, University of Sheffield.

Acknowledgements

The authors would like to thank everyone who has been involved with the production of this book, especially Dr Jon Scaife of the School of Education, University of Sheffield, for writing Chapter 8.

We gratefully acknowledge permission to reproduce material from:
Association of Graduate Careers Advisory Services for the table 'Differing Emphases in Three Types of CV' from the the AGCAS University Researchers and the Job Market publication.
Dr Lucy Lee of the University of Sheffield for the figure entitled 'Think Ahead Programme' from the article published in the *International Journal for Researcher Development*, Vol. 1, 2010, p. 280, figure 3.
Economic and Social Research Council for a flowchart of the ethics review process from its 'Framework for Research Ethics', p. 38, Appendix B.
The Continuum International Publishing Group for a table on 'Main Types of Research Publication'.
The estate of the late Alan Rousseau for notes given to Adrian Eley, which included a figure on 'A model for Project Management'.
TMS Development International Ltd for a figure showing The Margerison–McCann Team Management Wheel.
Vitae for a figure of the Researcher Development Framework.

We gratefully acknowledge permission to reproduce podcasts from:
Dr Luke Desforges, Dr Rachael Elder, Dr Kay Guccione, Grace Hoskins, Dr Simon Keegan-Phipps, Dr Heather Mortiboys, Dr Steve Mounce, George Parsons, Dr Rhiannon Pursall, Dr Jon Scaife, Dr Michael Trikic, and Dr Sara Whiteley.

We also gratefully acknowledge help from colleagues at the University of Sheffield including:
Ian Geary, Department of Infection and Immunity, for drawing the book figures.
Emily Hopkinson, HR Adviser (Staff Development), for advice on staff development issues in Chapter 9.

Richard Hudson, Research and Innovation Services, for advice on the future of ECR funding in the absence of Roberts funding.

Jean Lazenby, Department of Infection and Immunity, for secretarial assistance.

Dr Anne Lee and Dr Angie Negrine, Research and Innovation Services, for help with obtaining data from ECRs at the University of Sheffield.

Dr Heather Sugden and David Jones, Research and Innovation Services, for advice and help with collating data for Chapter 6.

Dr Tom Lovewell, Postdoctoral Researcher, Department of Infection and Immunity, for giving feedback on Chapter 2.

Kevin Mahoney, Careers Advisor for Postgraduate Researchers and Contract Research Staff, for his help and advice on Chapter 9.

Dr Graham McElearney, Corporate Information and Computing Services, for recording the podcasts.

Gayle McKeachie, HR Adviser, Department of Human Resources, for help and advice on Chapters 3 and 7.

Professor Jon Sayers, Department of Infection and Immunity, for writing the section on Commercialising your Research, in Chapter 9.

We also acknowledge help from Cathee J. Phillips, Executive Director, National Postdoctoral Association, Washington, DC, USA.

Preface

Over a number of years, there has been a growing frustration over the low status that early career researchers have in institutions and how in many cases their needs have been overlooked both as individuals and at the institutional level. To try to remedy this situation, efforts have been made primarily by national bodies and guidance is now available on websites and for specific topics in the printed form. However, the abundance of information and the lack of a central online resource can make finding relevant content challenging. This was the main driver for writing this book which will allow early career researchers to be able to find all the relevant information in one text.

As the authors all work in a UK institution, the emphasis of the book relates primarily to what is happening in the UK. However, we have wherever possible also tried to include information on developments that have taken place in Europe, the USA and elsewhere to give a greater international perspective. The latter was an important factor in helping us create our working definition of an early career researcher which the rest of the content is based on. The idea of bringing authors together from different subject areas was to try to give a more balanced view of what may be important to researchers from across the disciplines so that the text would have a more general appeal.

We have used a number of different formats to relay information to the reader including scenarios which are usually factually based and illustrate in practical terms some of the important issues raised. We include Top Tips in certain chapters which lend themselves to that sort of prescriptive advice. We incorporate quotations, which we call Personal Issues, from early career researchers in Sheffield who attended a focus group to discuss some important themes which were of direct relevance to them. We also refer the reader to a series of podcasts which were specifically made to highlight some of the key themes discussed in this book.

Lastly, we have tried to write the text in a more engaging and less formal style to make it more appealing to read. We sincerely hope that we have had some success in this approach and that the reader finds the text not only to be of interest but also enjoyable. We would be grateful for any feedback where we have made errors or any omissions.

Foreword

Recent years have seen significant change in terms of the opportunities for career development and the support for Early Career Researchers (ECRs). For instance the Concordat to Support the Career Development of Researchers (http://www.researchconcordat.ac.uk/) recognised the need for well-trained, talented and motivated researchers and laid out a vision of working practices, roles and responsibilities to further the attractiveness, and sustainability of research careers in the UK.

A specific principle of the Concordat was that researchers share the responsibility for their careers and should proactively engage in their own personal and career development. Organisations such as RCUK are keen to maintain momentum in the implementation of the Concordat – indeed this is specifically mentioned in the RCUK Vision for research careers and diversity and the RCUK delivery plan 2011–2015.

As a result of the activities of Vitae and of the 'Roberts' funding, which is now embedded into postgraduate research fees and research grants, the HE sector as a whole is well placed to continue to develop the human resource represented by the ECR cohort. Feedback on this support is now available through surveys of researchers such as the Careers in Research Online Survey (CROS) which assist the sharing of good practice across the sector. The aggregate results of the 2011 survey indicated that progress is being made but much remains to be done and there will be variations locally across what is a very heterogeneous research sector. At the time of writing most respondents to CROS seem well-informed about issues related to their current employment and research, but less so about their potential progression.

The book should help ECRs to understand the contribution that their personal skills can make to their careers. It is important for researchers to recognise that these skills can contribute to their employability and impact in a wider range of roles both within and beyond academia.

This book should be of assistance to all those who are at the early stage of a research career and to those who are supporting them in their development.

Iain Cameron
Head, Research Careers and Diversity
Research Councils UK

Chapter 1

Introduction

This chapter will help to set your experience as an ECR in a global context, as we explore the policies and practices of different institutions to find an all-encompassing definition of what it means to be an early career researcher. We then discuss what your role might involve and the status you might have in your institution and within the academic community more widely. As the last few years have seen changes in the development of the ECR role and its support mechanisms, this is a timely moment to consider the drivers for these changes, and to think about what they might mean for your future career.

Starting out as an Early Career Researcher (ECR), you might be thinking about how your role fits within the academic community, not just of your department and institution, but of your discipline, and not just in your own country, but on a global scale. The term itself is relatively new but the concept of postdoctoral workers in the USA can be traced back to 1876 when the first president of Johns Hopkins University came up with the idea of offering $500 fellowships to a select group of 20 graduates interested in further studies of literature or science. Among this group were four men with doctoral degrees who therefore became the first postdocs.

It is estimated that there are approximately 90,000 ECRs in the USA and more than 30,000 in the UK, which must translate to a few hundred thousand world-wide (National Science Board 2008; Second Annual Report on Research Staff, Funders Forum 2009). However, despite these numbers, these researchers have largely been ignored in academic studies and there is little guidance published for them, hence the need for this book, which is aimed directly at you as an ECR, and at the mentors and other colleagues who will help to shape your experience and career.

What is an ECR?

Not that long ago there were fairly clear divisions between researchers at different stages throughout their career, starting with doctoral students then progressing to postdoctoral workers and finishing with academic staff. However, more recently throughout Europe and to an extent worldwide, the term Early Career Researcher (ECR) has been introduced, which overlaps all three stages although it primarily replaces those who were called postdoctoral workers. This has partly been a response to the increasing importance of researchers, which has been reflected by their increased respect and status shown by national, international and funding bodies.

As will be clear from this description, and perhaps from your own experience, an ECR does not automatically equate to a postdoctoral worker. Also, the term ECR is not universally accepted and there are alternative names which are used (Johnson 2009: 5). It has been pointed out that the lack of a consistent definition of postdoctoral workers or agreement on the precise nature of the population concerned has hampered research into the character of postdoctoral positions (Akerlind 2005: 25).

To set the scene, in the context of the Bologna process in Europe, doctoral education is the third cycle of higher education and the first stage of a new researcher's career. In Europe but outside of the UK, the term Early Stage Researcher (ESR) is Salzburg Principle no. 4 (a set of ten basic principles concerning doctoral programmes and research training); it is used to describe a PhD student and 'covers the first 4 years of experience in research or the period until a doctoral degree is obtained, whichever is shorter'. However, in the European Charter (European Commission 2005: 29) the situation becomes confused as Experienced Researchers

> are defined as researchers having at least four years of research experience (full-time equivalent) since gaining a university diploma giving them access to doctoral studies, in the country in which the degree/diploma was obtained, or researchers already in possession of a doctoral degree, regardless of the time taken to acquire it.

Therefore, by European terminology it is difficult to differentiate between ECRs and experienced researchers! Care must also be taken about using the terms Early Career Investigator (ECI) and Early Stage Investigator (ESI) as used in the USA. The National Institutes of Health (NIH) defines these as a person within 10 years of completing their terminal research degree or medical residency, which is likely to be very different to a doctoral student in the European context.

In the UK, the Arts and Humanities Research Council defines an ECR as someone 'within eight years of the award of your PhD or equivalent professional training or within six years of your first academic appointment'. In Australia, the Australian Research Council defines early career status as:

> An early career researcher is one who is currently within their first five years of academic or other research related employment allowing uninterrupted,

stable research development following completion of their postgraduate research training.

Similarly, in the USA for the Wickham Skinner Awards, the term ECR is used and is defined 'as someone who has received a doctoral degree within the previous six years'.

For the purpose of this book and to respect definitions worldwide, we will categorise ECRs as those researchers who range from senior doctoral students to postdoctoral workers who may have up to 10 years postdoctoral education; the latter group may therefore include early career or junior academics. The topics that we cover in the book should be relevant to you, whichever of these groups you fall in to – and they will also have implications for your mentor, supervisor or other colleagues as they work alongside you during this stage of your career.

Given the range of experience that many people bring to the role of ECR, you might feel most comfortable with the in-depth definition provided on its website by the National Postdoctoral Association of the USA, which states that

> a postdoctoral scholar ('postdoc') is an individual holding a doctoral degree who is engaged in a temporary period of mentored research and/or scholarly training for the purpose of acquiring the professional skills needed to pursue a career path of his or her choosing.
>
> (http://www.nationalpostdoc.org/policy/what-is-a-postdoc)

Role of an ECR

So why do academic institutions need ECRs? You might be asking yourself that question – or wanting to provide answers for those around you! There is no doubt that increasing the number of highly skilled researchers makes a significant contribution to the production of national and international knowledge and innovation. Moreover, in a global economy, society needs highly trained employees who are adaptable and mobile, and are able to work effectively in a variety of different contexts within and outside of academia, during their professional careers.

An example of the importance of postdoctoral experience is particularly highlighted in a cohort of biochemists from the USA during the 1980s in which

> a postdoc appointment is regarded as a necessary step after doctoral completion, whether the individual plans a career in academia or in the business, government or non profit sectors. Consequently, the postdoc, not the PhD, has become the general proving ground for academic excellence, scientific entrepreneurship, and ultimate intellectual independence.
>
> (*Science* 1999: 1533)

However, more recent research (Brown, Lauder, and Ashton 2008) has challenged the direct link between economic success and education. Emerging economies such as India and China are rapidly building up their education system so that high-skill people in low-cost countries become an attractive option for multinational companies. This could result in a situation where young people in developed countries who are investing heavily in their education, may struggle to find employment in the careers to which they aspire. It would appear that it is timely to debate the future of education and skills and their relationship to careers, prosperity and social justice in a global economy. The days of assuming that higher levels of education will automatically lead to success in the global job market are coming to an end.

Not so long ago when there were fewer ECRs around, a large proportion would have gained future employment in universities. However, this situation has changed considerably and in contrast, the majority of ECRs will not take up academic positions. As we discuss in later chapters, your own perspective on this might affect your decisions about how to prioritise your efforts during your ECR years – your decisions about whether (and where) to publish, for example, will assume different significance according to your future prospects.

Historically most universities have not maintained very accurate records of the numbers of ECRs on campus, and although that situation is changing, it is still difficult to obtain data on how ECRs progress in their career, and instead we have to rely on data on career destination and progression of doctoral graduates.

In a recent UK study of the first employment destinations of doctoral graduates from 2003–2007, 35% went into research roles across all sectors, with higher education being the main destination where 23% of all respondents were employed as research staff and 14% as lecturers (Vitae 2009a). Similarly, in related publications looking at career profiles of doctoral graduates (where almost 70% were from science or engineering backgrounds), less than half of graduates across all subject areas were employed in the education sector (Vitae 2009b; Vitae 2010a). Obviously, this means that a large number of ECRs will not be employed in academia – some through the choice of a different career path and others after a disappointing period of applying for a limited number of academic jobs. In a time of uncertain academic employment, it might be encouraging to remember that as an ECR you will gain many generic and transferable skills, which you can benefit from in a more varied job market (Figure 1.1).

Status of an ECR

Concerns with postdoctoral research training and employment outcomes have been growing at an international level and have included increasing dissatisfaction among postdoctoral workers with the nature of their position (Akerlind 2005: 1). Similarly, in a review of the postdoctoral system in the USA, postdoctoral researchers were described as 'in a kind of limbo between student and independent researcher, without the status that their peers in other

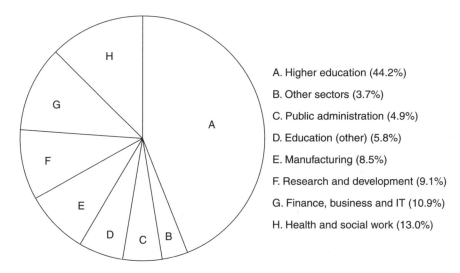

A. Higher education (44.2%)

B. Other sectors (3.7%)

C. Public administration (4.9%)

D. Education (other) (5.8%)

E. Manufacturing (8.5%)

F. Research and development (9.1%)

G. Finance, business and IT (10.9%)

H. Health and social work (13.0%)

Figure 1.1 Employment sectors for all doctoral graduate respondents in UK employment (November 2008). From Vitae (2010a) *What do researchers do? Doctoral graduate destinations and impact three years on* (p. 15).

professions enjoy' (Mervis 1999: 1513). However, in 2009, the NIH announced a new policy (NOT-OD-09-021) designed to encourage early transition to research independence. In a study of postdoctoral fellows in Canada, a key area of concern was the low value placed on postdoctoral researchers by institutions (Helbing, Verhoef, and Wellington 1998). It is clear therefore, that many postdoctoral researchers have status concerns and this has been highlighted in a recent European report (European University Association 2007: 30) where more countries did not recognise the status officially than those that did.

In an Australian example, gaining and maintaining research council large-grant funding for one's own research is the most significant hurdle to overcome in becoming established and accepted as a career researcher in academia (Bazeley 2003: 269). Knowing what information is used to assess ECR status can be helpful in planning your own strategy for success, and Bazeley (2003: 275) outlines these as follows:

- research qualification;
- year in which research qualification was obtained;
- current position, including year and level of appointment;
- year of first non-casual appointment to an academic institution;
- year of first non-casual appointment in the current place of employment;
- significant periods of absence from a research environment after qualifying with PhD;

- number, duration and type of research fellowships which have been held;
- position with respect to grants held during past 5 years;
- research output during the last 5 years.

The implication here is that excellent performance in the above will more likely lead to independent researcher status and academic positions.

The European Charter for Researchers (European Commission 2005: 27) makes the following statement:

> Clear rules and explicit guidelines for the recruitment and appointment of postdoctoral researchers, including the maximum duration and the objectives of such appointments, should be established by the institutions appointing postdoctoral researchers. Such guidelines should take into account time spent in prior postdoctoral appointments at other institutions and take into consideration that the postdoctoral status should be transitional, with the primary purpose of providing additional professional development opportunities for a research career in the context of long-term career prospects.

In the UK a significant development in employment law is discussed in detail in the University and College Union's (UCU) *The Researchers' Survival Guide*, which refers to The Fixed-Term Employees (Prevention of Less Favourable Treatment) Regulations 2002 (University and College Union 2008). Essentially this means that staff such as ECRs on fixed-term contracts (sometimes also known as contract research staff) must be treated no less favourably than comparable members of staff. This applies to contractual terms such as pay and annual leave but also representation in university committees and governance. A significant improvement has been in the nature of contracts awarded to longer-serving employees. Now ECRs have the right to regard their position as permanent if the following conditions are met:

- The employee is on at least their second contract with the same employer or the contract has been previously renewed.
- The employee has at least 4 year's continuous service.
- The use of a fixed-term contract was not justified on objective grounds.

Unfortunately, in the UK and despite the above improvements, a significant issue was the status of the ECR in the previous Research Assessment Exercises [RAE] (which determined institutional research income). In the RAE of 2008, ECRs could only be included in the institution's submission if they showed independence, which was generally interpreted as having a fellowship, together with research papers of sufficient calibre. Using these criteria, the majority of ECRs would not be submitted, despite being at the very centre of academic research. It is no surprise that the requirement to publish high quality papers within a fairly short timescale is particularly problematic as contracts are typically short. In later chapters on writing and publishing, we will feature the views of some of our ECR focus group participants, who have experienced a range of difficulties and successes in this area.

At the moment, the situation is unlikely to change for the Research Excellence Framework (REF), which has replaced the RAE as the new system for assessing the quality of research in UK higher education institutions, and should be completed in 2014. At the time of writing, no decision has been made on whether the research output of the ECRs will be submitted. Even if ECRs are submitted, those that work in disciplines where the new idea of using citation information as a marker of research quality will be disadvantaged further, as citation indexes can only be compiled once papers have been published, placing additional pressure on publication times. Your mentor will be able to advise you on the latest information regarding these decisions, and on their implications for your research activities. You will no doubt share our view that ECRs' research should be valued and acknowledged through REF submission, if you are to be made to feel fully part of your department and your discipline.

Roles within different disciplines

As you embark on your first ECR post, you will be aware of the multiple strands of your new postdoctoral existence, including the need to establish a professional identity and develop into an independent researcher, competing for grants and increasing one's output of research publications. ECRs may perform many different tasks, as shown in a meta-analysis (James, Norman, De Baets, *et al.* 2009: 13), but your roles and expectations will be shaped in part by your subject area. For example, in sciences and engineering, ECRs are commonly part of a large research team and often have to work in collaborative groups. This necessitates demands on interpersonal skills and can lead to tension in the interaction with your supervisor or mentor. In contrast, in the arts and humanities and perhaps the social sciences, an ECR is more likely to be an independent scholar with a requirement to work alone. This often leads to a different type of relationship (but not necessarily any less stressful) with your supervisor or mentor.

Scenario 1.1 – A tale of two disciplines

Martin had a successful research career after obtaining an excellent first degree, followed by a PhD in Molecular Biosciences. He was then able to gain postdoctoral experience with a 2-year spell in the USA, after which he spent a further 3 years as a research fellow in the UK. When his dream position as a junior academic in the Department of Molecular Biosciences was advertised, he was a strong contender as his 5 years of post-PhD research experience gave him a significant advantage over candidates who had held only one 2- or 3-year post, and had not worked in two different research environments.

A similar junior academic vacancy also arose at the same university but in Italian. Jenny had been keen on languages since secondary school and went on to take a joint honours degree in French and Italian which she passed with flying colours. After a successful time studying for a research Masters degree, she duly went on to obtain her doctorate in modern Italian literature. However, in contrast to the sciences, there are few postdoctoral research fellowships in the arts and humanities available in the UK, and despite the fact that she was an excellent candidate, she was unsuccessful in obtaining such a research post. Nevertheless, Jenny was undeterred and managed to continue to pursue her research independently by obtaining a short-term teaching-only position at another university, which gave her access to all the research facilities she needed. This resourcefulness proved to be just what the Department of Italian was looking for, and Jenny was short-listed for the academic vacancy.

Drivers for change

In the USA, where perhaps most developments with postdoctoral researchers have taken place, during the last 20 years or so, disillusioned postdocs got together at research institutions and national laboratories to push for institutional change. These changes included improved salaries, benefits, career training and protection against exploitation. More recently, postdocs realised that they needed to push for reforms nationwide and not just in their local institutions. Such a group of postdocs met in 1998 and proposed the following recommendations (Ferber 1999: 1516):

1. A written contract

Agreed upon in writing by postdoc, supervisor, and host institution, the contract would ensure that principal investigators and universities comply with federal laws on family leave, harassment, and discrimination based on race, gender, age, or disability; that postdoc performance be evaluated annually and in writing; and that universities provide formal grievance procedures for postdocs.

2. Uniform job title and benefits

Regardless of source of funding or academic department, all postdocs at a given institution should have the same job title, and that title should not be shared by non-PhD technicians or graduate students.

3. Postdoctoral associations

Universities should support either a postdoctoral association or central postdoctoral office, which would conduct a survey to gauge the needs of postdocs, offer an orientation and a manual for new postdocs, and provide courses on science survival skills such as writing grants and research papers and landing a job. [1]

Scenario 1.2 – The importance of a local postdoctoral association

It had all been a bit of a rush but Jane had been offered and accepted a position to work with Dr. Angers at very short notice. At least she hadn't got to move very far from her previous institution. Jane was very excited about the work ahead but when she arrived at the new institution, no-one seemed very clear about what she should be doing, and not very helpfully, Dr. Angers had just left to visit some collaborators overseas. Still, there were plenty of practical things to arrange and sort out such as getting to grips with the geographical peculiarities of the institution and how to acquaint oneself with safety issues, including out of hours training. Jane by nature was a fairly easy-going person but found it very stressful trying to get little jobs done with no real support. Yes, fellow ECRs at the new institution and members of staff tried to do their best to help out but there did not appear to be a system for guiding new ECRs like Jane through this frustrating early stage. She began to think that a lack of support which created a lot of unnecessary work was a very inefficient use of her time and did not create a good impression of how the institution valued its ECRs. She would certainly let Dr. Angers know what she thought of the present set-up on his return.

It could all have been so much easier for Jane if the institution had a local postdoctoral association. First, there would be helpful contacts; second, there would be verbal and well as published guidance on a whole range of relevant matters; and third, there would be a system already in place to welcome and support ECRs from the beginning. Not only that, she could if she wished share information and have discussions with like-minded colleagues on a whole range of issues. Moreover, once familiar with the association, she would be invited to a range of meetings and workshops to help develop her career. It would certainly have given her a good start and made her feel a valued employee.

---

4. Postdoc representation on institutional policy-making committees

National postdoctoral organisation

Funded by contributions from universities that train postdocs or federal agencies, the organisation would offer a postdoctoral voice in national science policy debates, support fair labour practices and salaries and benefits commensurate with their PhD, keep postdocs abreast of job trends, and help them identify funding sources for fellowships and research.

Since 2003 the National Postdoctoral Association (NPA) has provided a national voice for postdoctoral scholars in the USA. The association has assumed a leadership role in addressing the many issues confronting the postdoctoral community which require action beyond the local level. From the start the association worked collaboratively and constructively with research institutions, postdoctoral affairs offices, postdoctoral associations, professional organisations, and scientific funding agencies.

The association's mission is 'to advance the US research enterprise by maximising the effectiveness of the research community and enhancing the quality of the postdoctoral experience for all participants'.

In Europe the situation is a little different. Although EURODOC calls itself the European-wide federation of national associations of PhD candidates, and more generally of young (but probably better to have said 'junior' as some ECRs are middle-aged and have returned to academia after a previous career elsewhere) researchers, its target audience is PhD candidates. However, some important guidance has been provided by the European Charter for Researchers and the Code of Conduct for the Recruitment of Researchers (European Commission 2005). This charter is a set of general principles and requirements which specifies the roles, responsibilities and entitlements of researchers as well as employers and/or funders of researchers.

In the UK a more practical innovation saw the first national organisation to be developed in 2008 to promote the professional and career development of both doctoral researchers and research staff (including ECRs) in higher education institutions and research institutes. The organisation is called Vitae, is funded by Research Councils UK (RCUK) and has a programme of national activities, which includes the work of eight regional Hubs. Vitae has four key aims:

• Championing the development and implementation of effective policy;
• Enhancing higher education provision through sharing practice and resources;
• Providing access to development opportunities and resources;
• Building an evidence base to support the researcher development agenda.

Vitae have recently launched a major new approach to researcher development called the Researcher Development Framework [RDF] (Vitae 2010b). The RDF supports the implementation of the Concordat to Support the Career Development of Researchers (http://www.researchconcordat.ac.uk/), the QAA (2004) Code of practice for research degree programmes and the Roberts (2002) recommendations for postgraduate researchers and research staff. The latter developed from the Research Careers Initiative (Universities UK 2005) that began in 1997 and was augmented by the 1999 EC Fixed Term Work Directive (Council Directive 1999).

The structure of the RDF into four domains reflects empirical data collected through interviewing researchers to identify characteristics of what makes excellent researchers. These domains are:

- *Knowledge and intellectual abilities* – the knowledge, intellectual abilities and techniques to do research.
- *Personal effectiveness* – the personal qualities and approach to be an effective researcher.
- *Research governance and organisation* – the knowledge of the standards, requirements and professionalism to do research.
- *Engagement, influence and impact* – the knowledge and skills to work with others and ensure the wider impact of research.

The Vitae Researcher Development Framework enables you to articulate your skills and take a proactive approach to your own professional development: you might find it helpful as you progress through your first months or years in your role, for reflecting on your skills and your developmental needs.

In addition, Vitae also support the UK Research Staff Association which was established in 2010 to provide a collective voice for researchers (but not exclusively ECRs) at institutions across the UK. [2]

Eley and Murray (2009: 163) point out that in the UK, the contribution of ECRs to the supervision of research students is being increasingly recognised by institutions (probably as demands on academic staff increase) and funding bodies such as research councils. Similarly, in the USA a new law on science education (Lederman 2007) requires that applications for National Science Foundation (NSF) grants that include funds for ECRs have to describe the mentoring and professional development activities of ECRs, and require the NSF to evaluate those activities as a factor in the grant review process (see also Chapter 3).

University structure and organisation

Depending on your experience as an ECR and whether you have started at a new institution, the type and quantity of information on university structure and organisation that you need will vary according to circumstances. If you have become a junior member of academic staff you will very quickly need to acquire a good understanding, especially as knowledge of the university administration system will become vital for your everyday activities. Until recently, most ECRs have not received an induction session although these are now becoming more common. Ideally, you should be offered an induction session, similar to that offered to academic staff, which gives basic advice and information relating to the fundamental structure of an institution so that you will be able to function to your best advantage. Information to ask for, if this has not been provided, includes:

- details of Departmental/School, Faculty and University Research Committees;
- details of Departmental/School, Faculty and University Teaching Committees;
- details of the University and/or Faculty Postdoctoral Associations/ Committees;
- information on the institution's research office such as who to contact for all aspects of funding, commercialisation, ethics and governance;
- student support including counselling and possibly English Language Teaching;
- IT, technical and secretarial support;
- careers;
- library facilities;
- safety services;
- Human Resources.

Equally, it is useful to have a good knowledge and understanding of key personnel such as the Vice-Chancellor and Pro-Vice-Chancellors who make up the University Executive Board, Deans and Associate Deans of Faculty, Directors of Research, Directors of Teaching and Directors of the Graduate School as well as Heads of Departments (both academic and non-academic such as Human Resources). The above terminology relates to posts that are found in the UK but there will be institutional variations. In the USA, titles differ, with the President or Chancellor running the university and Pro-Vice-Chancellor equivalents being called Provost or Vice President. The term Vice President is likely to replace what we would probably refer to as Directors in the UK. The equivalent Head of Department title is known as Departmental Chair.

Content of remaining chapters

This chapter has served as a general introduction, intended to locate your own experience of being an ECR within a broader context. In the next chapter we will discuss how to choose a research topic (Chapter 2), including the advantages and disadvantages of developing a research interest in the topic of your doctoral degree; we will also reflect on the importance of team working and resources. Chapter 3 will concentrate on the importance of choosing a mentor and whether that means a well-known and distinguished academic or someone more junior. This chapter will also discuss the role of a mentor and how that might differ from that of a supervisor. How to develop research writing is the topic of Chapter 4, as the ability to develop your writing can have a direct effect on whether a completed piece of research work is of publishable quality; strategies to improve your writing are also discussed. Similarly, Chapter 5 discusses how to get research published in the best quality publications and the differences between publishing in journals and books. Chapter 6 concentrates on how best to apply for research funding; tips will be given on how to write a good quality application and to be successful in obtaining these awards. In Chapter 7 we will look at the important topic of how to develop as a research supervisor and in so doing recognise differences between the disciplines. We will also discuss project management as well as ethics, governance, research integrity, work-related stress, bullying and harassment. As for the majority, teaching is likely to be included in the ECR job description we will focus on becoming a teacher in Chapter 8. This will include a discussion of teaching methods including alternative approaches to teaching which may become more relevant in an ever-changing higher education environment. Career development will be the topic of Chapter 9 as it is important to know how to promote yourself in your academic field, how to make a successful job application and how to succeed in a job interview. We will also take note of Concordats, Charters and Associations worldwide to enhance and promote careers of ECRs. Finally, in Chapter 10 we will bring together our conclusions, suggest future directions and aspirations, and how these may affect your role and that of ECRs in general.

Terminology

Although written by academics in the UK, we would like this book to be of interest to colleagues around the globe. To go some way towards achieving this aim, we try to use generic terms when we can. For example, when we talk of junior academics we mean lecturers in the UK and assistant professors in the USA. Of course, it is not possible to include examples for every country, but we ask the reader to appreciate that we try to use suitable, generic terminology wherever possible.

Summary

There is no doubt that the status of ECRs has changed significantly over the last twenty or so years and that these changes continue for the better. However, there is still progress to be made and considerable advantages have been seen with the creation of institutional, national and international postdoctoral associations, which in turn have led to more drivers for change.

Increasingly, ECRs are less likely to become academic members of staff and alternative careers should be sought that may or may not be associated with research.

Recommended/Further reading/Links

http://www.vitae.ac.uk

The Vitae website provides a considerable amount of information on the personal, professional and career development of ECRs in the UK.

http://www.nationalpostdoc.org

The National Postdoctoral Association of the USA website develops and provides resources that postdocs and administrators need for success. It also provides opportunities for the postdoctoral community to connect.

Chapter 2

Choosing a research topic

The decision about choosing which research topic to follow is often a difficult one and some might say that interest in the research area should outweigh all other considerations, including topicality, research mentor and funding. However, the choice of topic can have a significant effect on one's career prospects. Perhaps a fallback position is to change research topics if things just don't work out? But is that feasible in today's competitive market and even if that was possible, wouldn't the previous research work feel like a waste of time?

So, why should you really have to consider choosing a research topic when you have already been working in a research field for several years whilst studying for your doctorate? In some ways the answer is a simple one. Undertaking a doctorate is fundamentally about the process of becoming an independent researcher and therefore acquiring research expertise cannot be considered a waste of time, even when the subject area of study changes. In other words, this was an opportunity to acquire and develop research skills whilst pursuing a research degree. So when you were awarded a doctorate, during the process you gained considerable expertise in your particular chosen field, i.e. the doctoral experience is as much about the process as the product (Wellington 2010: 78–79). Nevertheless, when you begin to be taken seriously in a particular research field, it could be rather daunting thinking about moving into a different research area, although this will broaden research skills and provide opportunities for additional training.

Perhaps the first consideration should be why you decided to work in your particular research field for your doctorate. Most of these points are still relevant to postdoctoral study. Five tips on choosing a research area for your doctorate as described by the University of Sussex (www.sussex.ac.uk/aboutus/schoolsdepartments/doctoralschool/researchdegrees/) are given below:

1   *Don't be too ambitious* – the realisation is that the project has to produce an original contribution to knowledge within a set timeframe.

2   *Think about your previous experience* – your choice might be influenced by a subject you enjoyed at undergraduate and/or postgraduate level and quite possibly by the person that taught it.

3   *Look at emerging research areas* – this is perhaps more difficult for a prospective doctoral student. However, keeping abreast of recent publications and discussions with academic staff should help in this regard.

4   *What are the hot topics for society, government and the media?* Increasingly, resources are being targeted in certain areas as university research has to show its impact on society and the economy. Choosing one of these areas may influence greater chances of obtaining research funding.

5   *Always remember you can change direction once you have started.* It is often true that the completed thesis may be somewhat different from how it might have been imagined at the beginning of the research. However, in some subject areas, funding is aligned with the research topic, so that little deviation is allowed from the original research proposal.

There are also significant differences between disciplines in how doctoral research projects are chosen. In science and engineering, students usually choose a research project that has been initially proposed by the supervisor as it builds on their own area of research expertise. In arts and humanities, the student more often creates the research proposal and then afterwards looks to find the best academic available who could supervise the project. Moreover, in the social sciences and arts and humanities, it is likely that the research proposal is more developed giving a clearer outline of the proposed research area as well as including key research questions, possible methodologies and gaps in the current literature that need filling. In contrast, the research proposal is often not as detailed in science and engineering (Wellington 2010: 24–25) unless they have been funded by research councils or other funding bodies that require clear outlines and ask specific research questions.

An overview of the process of addressing the research question for a doctorate is shown in Wisker (2005: 87).

Choosing a research topic after your doctorate

Although we will try to generalise here, it is appreciated that, for some researchers (such as junior ECRs, perhaps in their first postdoctoral position whose aim is primarily to broaden their experience), the reasons for choosing a research topic may be different from a junior academic perhaps with several years' experience, who is wanting to establish and develop their own research field.

As we discuss above, you have already made a number of choices to determine in which research field you wished to pursue your doctorate. Perhaps not surprisingly, the majority of doctoral students generally continue to develop their research in the same field (Johnson 2009). Nevertheless, this is the big opportunity to reflect on what you would like to do for the rest of your career and as

Yewdell (2008) states, 'in many ways the most important decision on the Principal Investigator (PI) career path is where you do your postdoctoral fellowship'. Similarly, Reis (1999) states, 'of all the decisions you'll make as an emerging scientist, none is more important than identifying the right research area, and in particular, the right research topic. Your career success will be determined by those two choices'. We believe this quotation is equally applicable to non-scientists too, whose careers will be shaped by the subject area they become identified with, and the people who mentor and collaborate with them in the years after the PhD.

Some fundamental thoughts on choice have been proposed by Doughty (http://www.anu.edu.au/BoZo/Scott/DoughtyProject.html) and Jones (2003). They consider that one possible step forward is to focus on an answerable and relevant research question. Jones (2003) goes further and suggests testing and refining the research question. In helping to assess a research area he also highlights the importance of novelty, relevance and likely impact, feasibility, fundability, whether publishable or not and ethical issues.

Doughty reminds us that you really need to be sure what type of research you like doing. He also points out what Loehle (1990) calls the Medawar Zone, named after Sir Peter Medawar, a Nobel prize-winning medical researcher (see also Chapter 4). This zone refers to the middle area (Figure 2.1) that yields a high payoff of discovery with a moderate degree of difficulty and is therefore desirable. Contrast this with solving an easy problem that has a low pay off because it is easily within reach and makes no great advance. Equally less desirable is trying to solve a very difficult problem that has a high potential payoff but is usually so

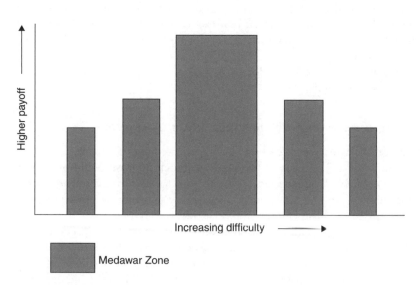

Figure 2.1 The Medawar Zone. Adapted from Loehle (1990).

difficult that there is often no payoff at all. In order to hit the Medawar Zone the best solution is to be well informed so that gaps in research knowledge can be identified and explored.

There is no doubt that choice of research environment is an important consideration especially with levels of research funding and the nature of the line manager or mentor. As Bettmann (2009) highlights, a clear overlap exists between choosing a research field, project, or laboratory and choosing a research mentor. This is appreciated and we say more about choosing a research mentor in Chapter 3. Bettmann (2009) also raises another important point about being neither too independent nor too dependent in research activities. It is good to have one's own research ideas and plans but it is also good at this relatively early stage in one's career to listen and take advice from more experienced academics.

Of course, we realise that trying to predict a research area that is going to be topical in the future is a difficult thing to do. If a particular field seems to have been fully explored, then its useful life may be limited. Secondly, a research topic may be so popular that everyone wants to work in that field and that could put serious restrictions on available funding. Thirdly, a research field may be new and exciting but not fully accepted by funding bodies and peers so that it is difficult to make a strong case for support in a field of uncertainty. One way of trying to identify a current research trend is through Scopus at www.Scopus.com. Scopus is a database of abstracts and citations for scholarly journal articles. It covers nearly 18,000 titles from more than 5,000 international publishers including coverage of 16,500 peer-reviewed journals in the scientific, technical, medical and social sciences (including arts and humanities) fields. However, it is owned by Elsevier and this potentially could lead to a conflict of interest in the choice of the periodicals to be included in the database.

Switching/changing

Unlike a doctoral project (and even then it can be a worry), it's generally not a good idea to change research topics midway through one's career as you could find yourself with no track record including publications in your new research topic, which means by and large that you are back to the doctoral stage again in terms of specific research experience. This could be seriously detrimental when trying to obtain grants as grant awarding bodies like to see a growing body of publications in one's field to establish credibility. Exceptions to this are the 'blue sky' projects sometimes funded by research councils, where a new research area is emerging and there are no existing experts: though even then, your track record within your own subject area will be used as a measure of your research skills and potential. Therefore, this all puts more pressure on making you try to get the decision right first time on your choice of research topic.

What we discuss above refers to an ideal situation where you wish and are able to obtain the position you really wanted. However, this will not always be the case and there will be situations where, for example, your funding runs out, possibly unexpectedly and you will be looking for another position. So what happens in these situations and how easy will it be then to obtain an ECR position, possibly by switching to other project areas? In some ways that depends on a number of factors such as whether you are prepared to move to any geographical location, whether you have family commitments that may tie you to one place and what your long term goals are. Other factors include the breadth of experience you have, which means you need to identify what your core skills are that could be transferable to other topic areas to make you more attractive to hire. Another consideration is whether you have a wide range of professional contacts to give you more opportunities. So the answer to the question is that, depending on personal circumstances, it can be very difficult when one is forced to consider moving to new project areas and this is one of the disadvantages of working as an ECR. Nevertheless, although our general advice on choosing a research topic may not be helpful to all situations, some of the basic principles still apply.

Some other major considerations in choosing a research project include the advantages of working in teams, an awareness of requirements for successful project management, acquiring access to and availability of resources, and an understanding of a number of other relevant issues including ethics and research governance.

Teams

For a variety of reasons, team working or working in groups of people either within and/or across institutions has become more common. In science and engineering, team working has always been more widely accepted, but the increase in team working has also been seen in social sciences and arts and humanities. A recent study looking at papers published and patent proposals over five decades has demonstrated that teams increasingly dominate solo authors in science and engineering, social sciences and arts and humanities (Wuchty, Jones, and Uzzi 2007). These authors also found that teams typically produce more frequently cited research than individuals and that this advantage has been increasing over time. Moreover, in general, teams now produce the exceptionally high impact factor research. The trend in the increasing development of research groups across the disciplines has also been recognised by Delamont and Atkinson (2004: 39). They state that it:

> reflects institutional pressures to concentrate research and present it to the outside world selectively, capitalizing on departmental and institutional strengths. It reflects the logic of the Research Assessment Exercise (now replaced by the REF), in which critical mass of researchers in sub-fields of research has been important. It should and could also reflect the benefits to be gained from collective commitments to research and its planning.

An important role for teams is to work together on the preparation of research bids for funding and the design of the research proposals that underpin them. A classic example for researchers in Europe is the response to European Framework Programme calls, which in some cases can involve research groups from ten or more institutions. Of course, a large consortium could appear daunting to an ECR who seeks to establish their own research field. Such a consortium might also be difficult at first to break into. An alternative approach might be to join a smaller consortium in the initial stages and hopefully as the research progresses, invitations to join larger consortia might follow.

A further significant and more recent development has been the encouragement of interdisciplinary teams to provide new opportunities of solving long-standing problems. This development reflects the increasing emphasis placed by the research councils and other funding bodies on larger-scale interdisciplinary projects focused on areas of societal and economic need. Such projects often address high-risk ground-breaking interdisciplinary research topics that are likely to open new avenues of research and new interdisciplinary collaborations.

However, it should be remembered that many of us have little or no training or experience on how to work efficiently in a team, and that key aspects of good teamwork should be worked at and acknowledged (Rousseau and Eley 2010: 10). When collaborating, it may be particularly useful to enter into some sort of agreement so that all parties are aware of their obligations. Several areas that collaborators should discuss are as described in the Burroughs Wellcome Fund and Howard Hughes Medical Institute (2006: 204) guide:

• the purpose of the collaboration;
• the scope of work;
• the expected contribution of each collaborator;
• financial responsibilities of each collaborator;
• milestones;
• reporting obligations;
• expectations about authorship.

Project management

Although knowledge of project management in itself won't necessarily help in the choice of a research topic, it will allow a greater understanding of what work on a research project will entail. Therefore, please refer to Chapter 7 where we discuss goal setting, PERT and Gantt Charting.

Similarly, one needs to have an awareness of increasing demands for ethical approval for a whole range of research projects and the way in which institutions manage research governance. Such knowledge can influence the time and other resources required to undertake certain aspects of research. These topics are also discussed in more detail in Chapter 7.

Resources

The relevance of this topic very much depends on which discipline you will be working in. Typically, in sciences and engineering, one commonly needs access to very specialised and often expensive equipment. If certain facilities are not available then this can certainly determine what sort of research is done in-house and what might need to be done by collaborators. Many institutions have reputations for doing certain types of work and the attraction of highly specialised facilities may be obvious targets for employment, depending on the nature of the chosen research project. In the arts and humanities and social sciences, the above facilities and equipment are not usually that important. Instead, access to world-class library facilities and special collections might be more of an issue together with particular computing and electronic resources.

Depending on the institution, junior academics may be offered start-up packages to enable the research work to be initiated and become more fully established without the immediate need to obtain research grants once in post.

Although perhaps more difficult to determine, knowledge of future plans (if known) for the Department, Faculty and institution could have serious implications for future research activities and may influence decisions as to which universities to pursue.

Lastly, it is important to be aware of areas that the national and international funding bodies are supporting and/or likely to support in the future.

Scenario 2.1 – When is it the right time to choose a research topic that is different to that of your doctorate?

Simon was coming towards the end of his PhD and was starting to think seriously about his future. On reflection, he had really enjoyed doing the research and even though he realised that it was going to be tough to obtain an academic position, certainly for the moment he wanted to develop as an ECR. He remembered that when he was looking for a research studentship, he had restricted his opportunities by only considering projects from the university where he had been an undergraduate. But then this had the advantage that he already knew the academic who was offering the project, and as he had always got on well with him, it was an easy decision when he was offered the post to accept it. However, in recent discussions with other members of his supervisory team, it had been made clear to him that there would probably be many advantages in trying to find a position at another institution, especially as he had been at the same university for both undergraduate and postgraduate studies. This got Simon thinking about possibly going to the USA as he thought this might be fun and certainly a lot different from where he was now. So the question was, how should he proceed to find a position elsewhere, possibly in the USA?

This is an interesting example which raises many issues. Simon is obviously keen to continue with his research and even though this will be his first position as an ECR, he has stated that he would like to become an academic. Therefore, potentially his decisions now could have long-lasting consequences. Even though Simon has some publications, is starting to get known in the field, and through conferences has got to know several big names in his current research area, he really needs to think in-depth about whether his current research topic will last the course, as he could be working on it for 30 years or more. If he is really sure that he would like to pursue the same research topic, then he should explore many of the big names in the field to see whether they might be able to offer him something. Whether this happens to be in the USA or not should be irrelevant. Greater importance should be placed on other factors such as the quality of research being undertaken, what sort of relationship the current research team has with the PI, the resources overall and the nature of the research project being offered. On the other hand, if Simon really believes that he should consider changing his research topic, then he needs to broaden his horizons and seek advice from others. It would almost certainly be beneficial to weigh up the pros and cons of a number of options before deciding on what will turn out to be life-changing events.

Scenario 2.2 – Whose research is it anyway?

Jenny had been appointed as Lecturer in the Department of Spanish and at her appointment interview was keen to discuss her major research topic in late medieval studies and what she had got planned for the future, in terms of research activities. Although not a major interest of hers, she also happened to comment on her time spent as a postdoc when she had become involved with and contributed to a book on the literature of Central America. At the interview this had certainly interested the Head of Department, Prof. Green, who was an authority on Central American literature and this was probably a factor in Jenny getting the job, although the departmental requirement was for a person with expertise in medieval studies.

Jenny was very excited about developing her research in medieval studies, had been working on some new lines of enquiry and was about to submit a major grant application when Prof. Green called her into her office. There was great news for Prof. Green as she had just been appointed Dean of Faculty and she was very excited about this new challenge. However, there was a problem in that she would not be able to spend much time on her major research topic and she was desperate to keep this work going. So she instructed Jenny to drop her current research activities and to help keep Prof. Green's research activities going which would include supervising a PhD student in Central American literature. Jenny was devastated. She thought she had been appointed to work in the field of medieval studies and she was very keen to make her name in that field. Admittedly, she had some limited experience in Central American literature but she had no desire to pursue these activities. What was she to do?

Perhaps the answer lies in the wording of the academic contract. It was true that Jenny had been appointed Lecturer in Medieval Studies but this was primarily to fill a teaching gap and although there was an expectation that she would do research in the same field, this was not explicit in the contract. However, what was written in the contract was that Jenny was to carry out reasonable duties as specified by the Head of Department. So although Jenny would feel justified in feeling upset at what Prof. Green had requested, her justification for asking her to do other research activities was as Prof. Green put it, 'for the good of the department' and in any case would only be for a period of 2 years. Of course, there is also the opportunity that by working in a different research area, Jenny would gain new experiences which may allow her to use similar methodologies and approaches in her own research.

Summary

The choice of research topic is one of the most important factors which can shape your career and should not be underestimated. It is also true that you need to have an awareness of the skills you can bring to a project and use that awareness to provide some flexibility when trying to match up project proposals. The ability to work in or part of a team, irrespective of subject area and geographical barriers seems to be advantageous in getting papers published and in attracting grant funding. However, several key issues need to be considered when embarking on a collaborative project.

Recommended/Further reading

Bourne, P. E. and Friedberg, I. (2006) Ten simple rules for selecting a postdoctoral position. *PLoS Computational Biology* 2: 1327–1328.
Although primarily written for scientists, these ten rules are also of relevance to non-scientists too and stimulate thoughts as to what to consider when choosing a postdoctoral position.

Chapter 3

Choosing a mentor

Perhaps the first question should be, does an ECR need a mentor and if so why? In trying to answer that question we will explore what it is we mean by mentoring and discover whether there is a difference between a supervisor and a mentor.

The first recorded mention of mentoring was about three thousand years ago and appeared in Homer's epic poem, *The Odyssey*. In Indo-European, 'men' means 'to think' and in ancient Greek, the word mentor means adviser. Therefore, a mentor is an adviser of thought (Garvey, Stokes, and Megginson 2009).

Firstly, it is important to understand what is meant by mentoring today. Paul Stokes, Senior Lecturer in Mentoring and Coaching at Sheffield Hallam University states:

> Mentoring is a one-to-one relationship between two people where, typically, one person (the mentor) helps the other (the mentee) in thinking through and taking action with regards to their life, work and career. The mentor is often more experienced than the mentee in thinking through their issues, challenges and aspirations. The mentor uses their accumulated wisdom skilfully by asking appropriate questions, offering stories based on their own experiences and, above all, placing the mentee's agenda at the centre of any mentoring conversation, by giving it their full attention. Ultimately, the mentee is responsible for their own life, work and career and uses the mentor as a sounding board and critical friend when deciding on what actions to take next. The learning agenda of the mentee is the primary focus for the relationship.
>
> (P. Stokes, personal communication, March 2011)

Not surprisingly, mentors have multiple responsibilities and according to the US Council of Graduate Schools, mentors are:

- Advisers – People with career experience willing to share their knowledge.
- Supporters – People who give emotional and moral encouragement.

- Tutors – People who give specific feedback on one's performance.
- Masters – Employers to whom one is apprenticed.
- Sponsors – Sources of information about opportunities and aid in obtaining them.
- Models of identity – The kind of person one should aspire to be as an academic or a professional scientist.

(Burroughs Wellcome Fund and Howard Hughes
Medical Institute 2006: 99)

However, although this provides a useful checklist in considering the role of the mentor, some aspects of this role, e.g. the master-apprentice model, have been criticised (Wellington 2010: chapter 4).

Different types of mentor

One thing that is clear when reading about the subject of mentoring is the confusion about how different bodies and institutions interpret what the role means to them and the different types of mentoring that are available (Table 3.1). Moreover, there is further confusion about how it can sometimes be mixed up with supervision. To progress further with this chapter, there needs to be a discussion of terminology and why we believe that the term mentor rather than supervisor is more appropriate to ECRs.

Much has been written on the role of the PhD supervisor but essentially teaching plays a big part in the supervisory process, ultimately leading to the development of independent researcher status of the student (Eley and Murray 2009; Rousseau and Eley 2010) although the question of whether a researcher should ever be totally independent or autonomous has been raised (Wellington 2010: 68–70). However, as the ECR has usually already achieved the PhD, is no longer an official student, and has developed into an independent researcher, what is required is advice rather than teaching. Moreover, the nature of the

Table 3.1 Different types of mentor for an early career researcher

Research mentor	Line manager, person responsible for project leadership
Mentor/adviser	Personal tutor, not directly involved with research programme
Clinical academic mentor	Clinical as well as academic guidance, similar to personal tutor role
Fellowship mentor	Senior academic providing support and leadership in place of line manager
Probation mentor	Senior academic within the same institution providing guidance to junior colleague
Society mentor	Senior academic from a different institution providing guidance

relationship has changed from teacher–student to senior/junior colleague. Therefore, in this chapter we will use the term mentor for a person who oversees and is responsible for the work of an ECR and reserve the term supervisor for a person who more closely directs and manages the work of a PhD student.

Unfortunately, the waters are muddied by the fact that in some parts of the world such as the USA, the term mentor can be used for a person who is supervising the PhD (Lee, Dennis, and Campbell 2007). That's not to say that the term mentor cannot be used for an academic who is helping a PhD student, but that for clarity, it might be helpful not to use that term for a principal supervisor.

The Burroughs Wellcome Fund and Howard Hughes Medical Institute (2006: 104) practical guide is particularly useful in this regard, as it makes clear that a major difference for ECRs is that they are in a state of transition. You are neither students nor complete professionals as often a period as an ECR is a prerequisite for an academic position. It also makes clear that you should be treated as collaborators and not students and should be allowed adequate independence to own your projects.

A recent personal reflection (Clarke 2004) of a junior academic observed the development of a layered relationship mentoring model. In this model, her mentoring experiences involved the following three phases:

1   Collegial friendship
2   Informal mentoring
3   Co-mentoring.

In the final phase, co-mentoring recognises the contribution that each phase brings to the relationship and is based on reciprocal benefit. Not surprisingly, this is important as the mentoring relationship will likely change for a new ECR if you develop into an academic, such that the latter phase will more likely lead to co-mentoring and is an obvious result of the development of the mentoring relationship.

A further confusion has originated from our own institution (Faculty of Medicine, Dentistry and Health, University of Sheffield). A new mentoring programme has been developed to provide personal and professional guidance to help support an ECR through all stages of their career in the Faculty and into their next position. Mentors are described as being members of academic staff but not their supervisor. This is an interesting development similar to the role of personal tutor or adviser for a PhD student as part of their supervisory team (Eley and Murray 2009: 71) but with a difference being that the mentor is more closely matched to a mentee in terms of suitable experience and expertise, and not just allocated as with a PhD student.

In the UK, Vitae (http:vitae.ac.uk/researchers/1310/Mentoring.html) also differentiate between 'informal mentoring' when a mentor offers advice and guidance in relation to a project or in career development and 'formal mentoring' which is often a recorded statement such as during a probationary interview. Key features of a formal mentoring relationship are:

- The mentoring relationship is confidential.
- Mentors and mentees are often required to attend training to help prepare them for the role.
- Mentoring usually takes place over an extended period of time, maybe 6 to 12 months.
- There will usually be a degree of choice over your mentor/mentee.
- There will be a named third person for you to contact if you are experiencing any problems with the mentoring arrangement.

Recently, the use of information technology and other media for mentoring conversations (so-called e-mentoring) have become increasingly popular (Garvey, Stokes, and Megginson 2009). Several benefits of e-mentoring have been proposed:

- It is less time consuming in terms of time off work and travel for mentors.
- It is easily accessible via the internet.
- It can help to equalize the power difference between mentor and mentee (as electronic communication is not influenced by factors characterised by a meeting).
- It removes first impression prejudice.
- It gives more time for reflection and learning.

However, of course, virtual mentoring does not offer the wide range of communication and information, such as non verbal messages, that is available in face-to-face mentoring. As the general use of e-mentoring is still relatively new, it remains to be seen if and how it may be developed in the future.

Mentoring requirements (mentor)

Until recently, mentoring arrangements were usually unstructured and left to the mentor. In some cases, mentors made an attempt to help in the personal and professional development of mentees, whereas with others, matters were very much left to the mentee to make the most of what they could themselves, with little or no support from the mentor. Obviously this was not a satisfactory situation and one response to it has come from the US National Science Foundation (NSF). The 2007 COMPETES Act now requires that all NSF grant proposals that include support for ECRs must contain a description of mentoring activities. Such activities must be contained in what is known as a Postdoctoral Researcher Mentoring Plan which would be reviewed as part of the grant proposal (http://www.natonalpostdoc.org/publications/mentoring-plans/mentoring-plan/223-nsf). In the 2009 NSF grant proposal guide, the need for a mentoring plan is described as:

Each proposal that requests funding to support postdoctoral researchers must include, as a supplementary document, a description of the mentoring activities that will be provided for such individuals. In no more than one page, the mentoring plan must describe the mentoring that will be provided to all postdoctoral researchers supported by the project, irrespective of whether they reside at the submitting organization, any subawardee organization, or at any organization participating in a simultaneously submitted collaborative project.

Examples of mentoring activities include, but are not limited to: career counseling; training in preparation of grant proposals; publications and presentations; guidance on ways to improve teaching and mentoring skills; guidance on how to effectively collaborate with researchers from diverse backgrounds and disciplinary areas; and training in responsible professional practices. The proposed mentoring activities will be evaluated as part of the merit review process under the Foundation's broader impacts merit review criterion. Proposals that include funding to support postdoctoral researchers, and do not include the requisite mentoring plan will be returned without review.

In some situations such as research labs, there may be the coming and working together of many individuals often including those from overseas. This means that a mentor needs to have an awareness of gender and cultural issues to avoid difficulties in communicating, which may then lead to misunderstandings and friction. One postdoc guide (Burroughs Wellcome Fund and Howard Hughes Medical Institute 2006: 108) advises on appropriate social behaviour of ECRs by recommending that the mentor:

- respects other people and does not offend them with jokes, pictures, or music that shows disrespect for who they are or where they come from;
- treats everyone fairly, and keeps the main focus on research;
- respects different sensitivities by tailoring ways of criticising students to their personal style;
- demonstrates a willingness to communicate with and understand each student, regardless of their background and culture.

In addition to the above, a mentor needs to be aware of issues that are particularly relevant to some such as women, minorities and the disabled. In this context it is advisable that the mentor is familiar with the institution's policies relating to discrimination and harassment (see also Chapter 7).

When working with overseas researchers, it is also advisable that a mentor has an awareness of cultural differences and that in certain cultures researchers are less likely to challenge senior colleagues but does not mean they do not have an opinion of their own.

The following table (Table 3.2), which has been adapted from Klasen and Clutterbuck (2002), shows some of the characteristics of a developmental

Table 3.2 Characteristics of a developmental mentoring process

At no time	Occasionally	At all times
Punitive	Using coaching behaviours	Listening and questioning with empathy
Performance management	Providing help and support	Sharing experience and learning
Supervision	Opening doors	Developing insight through reflection
Assessment for third party	Brokering or facilitating links	Being a sounding board and confidant
Disrespectful	Didactic	Professional and/or critical friendship Partnership Challenging Set up with specific outcomes intended

Note: Adapted from Klasen and Clutterbuck (2002).

mentoring process. However, we have some concerns over including supervision in the 'At no time' column, in that an element of supervision may always be needed in the mentoring process, just as total 'autonomy' or complete independence may not be an appropriate goal to strive for at any stage of one's career (Wellington 2010: 68–70).

Benefits of mentoring

Now that mentoring of ECRs is more commonplace and is becoming a requirement as outlined above, we should consider the potential benefits of the process. Guidelines from City University, London (http://www.city.ac.uk/sd/mentoringprofessional.html), state the following:

For the mentee:

- It aids induction into a new job and culture.
- It helps with developing skills, both professional and personal, in a structured way based on individual needs.
- It improves professional and personal networks.
- It provides an opportunity for a new member of staff to reflect on his/her own progress and resolve his/her problems in a confidential environment with someone other than their line manager.

For the mentor:

- It broadens his/her own skills and knowledge.
- It may provide a different dimension to his/her current job role.

- It brings new insights into the organisation.
- It enables him/her to demonstrate additional skills in developing other individuals.
- It consolidates and extends his/her professional and personal networks.

For the subject area:

- It breaks down hierarchical barriers.
- It improves communication across the area.
- It helps to develop identity of the area.

For the University:

- It facilities networking.
- It improves the transfer of learning.
- It helps develop diverse employees and remove barriers that may hinder their success.
- It can improve staff retention.

Mentoring meetings

Similar to supervisory meetings between PhD supervisor and student, often more formal meetings between mentor and mentee need a certain amount of preparation and organisation. City University, London (http://www.city.ac.uk/sd/mentoringprofessional.html) suggests the following:

The content of meetings should be negotiated between the mentor and mentee, and the mentor should be given time to prepare for the first meeting which should include:

- discussion of the mentoring guidelines;
- agreement on the future ways of working together – A Working Contract;
- location of meetings;
- frequency of meetings;
- scheduling of meetings;
- length of meetings;
- structure of the meetings.

Ground rules and boundaries including confidentiality on both sides and any limits to the role (for example, types of issues to be discussed, communication outside of meetings) should be discussed. Although some meetings may be more like conversations, others may be more structured. Likewise, the location of the meetings will be determined by their informality. The timing and frequency of meetings should be discussed and as the relationship develops, the frequency of meetings may change.

How to choose a mentor

Now that we have an idea of what mentoring is and what a good mentor can bring to a mentor–mentee relationship, you are in a position to contemplate what you might wish to consider when choosing a mentor.

As far as we are aware, every ECR has to have at least one type of mentor (see Table 3.1). Perhaps more often, the mentor will have obtained a grant to fund the researcher and he or she is required to work with the mentee on the project – a research mentor. Less commonly, an ECR will find their own funding to do research that is of prime interest to them. In this situation, a mentor will still be appointed but will not usually be as intimately connected with the research as in the first example (e.g. a fellowship mentor).

How to choose a research mentor

For the purpose of this discussion, we will assume that the mentor has obtained the funding and that the mentor is the prime person responsible for managing the project. So how do you choose a research mentor?

The answer is that it very much depends on what you want out of the research position. You might want to work with a 'big' name with the potential advantages that might bring (not forgetting the potential drawbacks such as difficulties in finding time for meetings and a lack of accessibility due to time spent away from the institution). You might want to work in a particular research field and the fame of the mentor is not that important to you. You might just want to further your career and in doing so identify the best possible mentor to work with in terms of their ability to build good working relationships whoever they work with. Ideally of course, you might want all three, but with the realisation that you are unlikely to meet a mentor that has all the qualities you are looking for. So the answer to the question is very much determined by what you consider to be important.

It's also noteworthy here to remember that being mentored is as relevant as mentoring. That means that the mentee needs to know what questions to ask and when, and know how to accept any advice they receive. In the long-term, the mentee should try to maintain personal and professional relationships with their mentor, which might help in obtaining career goals.

The Burroughs Wellcome Fund and Howard Hughes Medical Institute (2006: 107) guide to postdocs lists the following qualities to cultivate in learning how to be mentored well:

- *Foresight* – start early to think about your future.
- *Proactivity* – don't expect to be taken care of. You could easily be overlooked in the competitive world of research.
- *Probing* – ask tough questions. Find out about the experience of others with this potential mentor.

- *Respect* – be polite. Make and keep appointments. Stay focused. Don't over-stay your welcome.
- *Gratitude* – everyone likes to be thanked.
- *Reciprocation* – repay your mentor indirectly by helping others.
- *Humility* – be willing to accept critical feedback so that you are open to learning new ways of thinking about and doing research.

Accepting feedback is not as easy as it sounds, but to be really useful, you must listen – don't argue back, get defensive, or just hear what you want to hear. You need to remember that it is your mentor's perspective and not necessarily the truth, but it is what you asked for. If you want to go a bit deeper into this, it might be useful to consider the Johari Window. This model is a simple tool for illustrating and improving self-awareness and mutual understanding between individuals and was devised by American psychologists, Joseph Luft and Harry Ingham in 1955. Two key issues behind the model are that individuals can build trust with others by disclosing information about themselves, and that they can learn about themselves and come to terms with personal issues with the help of feedback from others.

Lastly, an article by Reis (2000) provides a useful discussion on choosing a research adviser (another name for line manager) and amongst other topics highlights three types of adviser, the collaborator, the one with the hands-off style, and the senior scientist, and what might be the best one for you.

How to choose a mentor/adviser

The major difference with this type of mentor in comparison to the research mentor is that you have no work responsibility to this person. This has both advantages and disadvantages. Perhaps the biggest advantage is the lack of work pressures including deadlines that could put a strain on the relationship between you and your research mentor. A potential disadvantage is a more likely lack of knowledge in the specific research field in which you are working. So the reason for choosing a mentor/adviser is to provide advice and guidance on one's longer term career development in a broad sense, rather than the specific feedback one would receive from a research mentor.

When choosing this type of mentor/adviser, experience would certainly be an important factor, together with an up-to-date knowledge of the pressures of the job, plus the ability, hopefully, to form a long-lasting relationship. Of course, proximity to the mentor/adviser could be an advantage but as your career is likely to involve working at several institutions, it has to be accepted that for a lot of the time, they may well be sited at another location. This is not necessarily a disadvantage as not being too close to your institution or to your research mentor, can help promote an unbiased and more objective opinion of how your career is progressing.

Of course, the above describes an ideal situation where you have a choice of mentor. However, this may not be the case in small departments and/or subject areas where there are very few potential mentors, and in these cases, one may have to compromise. With the development of institutional ECR mentoring plans, a possibility exists to have two mentor/advisers, one in your institution and one outside of it. Again, although this may be advantageous, and as we describe above, there are potential advantages and disadvantages of both. Moreover, depending on your career goals, the mentor/adviser does not have to work in a higher education institution but could alternatively work in a research institute or in industry/commerce.

Scenario 3.1 – How do you know you can work with your proposed research mentor?

Martina was coming to the end of her PhD research in the UK and although she wouldn't be able to submit her thesis for a few months, she was keen to try to obtain a postdoc position to further her research career. She was aware that a Prof. Bellamy from Australia who was one of the leading international names in her field was currently keen to recruit. Her problem was that even though she had briefly had an amicable meeting with Prof. Bellamy at a recent conference, he had a reputation of not only being a hard taskmaster but of also being a bit of a womaniser. Ideally, she would have liked to have visited his laboratory in Australia so she could see for herself what she could be letting herself in for, should she be offered a position. Prof. Bellamy understood Martina's concerns about not being able to visit his laboratory, but the deadline for the postdoc application was fast approaching and there just wouldn't be time to arrange a visit. What was Martina to do?

As Martina had discovered for herself, sometimes when one becomes particularly specialised, often the most appropriate postdoc positions are overseas, which at the time can sound very attractive, as in the case above. However, there are many issues to consider when contemplating working as a postdoc. Perhaps first and foremost, one really needs to try and find out whether a satisfactory working relationship with your proposed research mentor can be achieved. It might sound appealing career-wise working with a world authority but when they rarely have time to see you and are not particularly interested in your development, this can feel very unsatisfactory, especially if you are alone and thousands of miles from friends and family. There is no doubt that despite the travel distance, trying to arrange a visit to the mentor is essential. This would allow for discussions with potential postdoc colleagues to enable them to give their opinions of the mentor in confidence, as well as provide an assessment of research facilities and accommodation. If a visit is not a possibility, then a poor substitute would be a video conference (or possibly Skype), again especially if others such as current postdocs can be present, bearing in mind that the presence of the mentor will no doubt bias any discussions with them. So without a visit, Martina could discuss issues with her PhD supervisor depending on the nature of their relationship. She should request a video conference. She could also communicate with Prof. Bellamy's current and previous postdocs (although the latter might be more difficult to track down). Depending on the outcomes of the above, even if working with Prof. Bellamy sounds like a good idea, the final decision, if positive, would still require a leap of faith.

Scenario 3.2 – How to get the best out of the mentor–mentee relationship?

Hassan couldn't believe he was finally working in the US with Dr. Rogers. It had been Hassan's dream for so long and despite the bureaucratic nightmare of obtaining all documentation to work in the US, it had eventually come true. However, after only a few weeks Hassan became deeply unhappy. He seemed to have so many problems to resolve outside of the lab and to make matters worse, Dr. Rogers was becoming less and less friendly towards him. Hassan couldn't understand why even opening a bank account turned into such a big issue, and as for obtaining a local credit card, that seemed to be completely out of the question. The number of times he had told Dr. Rogers about all these domestic issues just seemed to get him nowhere, as Dr. Rogers after a while, seemed less and less interested in providing any assistance. In fact, on one occasion when Hassan had approached Dr. Rogers about his difficulties in arranging for a telephone connection to his apartment, Dr. Rogers seemed to have lost his temper with him and told him he was more interested as to why it was taking Hassan so long to complete some basic experiments in the lab. At this outburst Hassan was very upset indeed. So despite Hassan's dream having come true, all he could increasingly think about was going home.

The above is a classic scenario of different expectations on behalf of what the mentor and mentee should be having in their relationship. Even though Dr. Rogers is probably a reasonable and understanding mentor, it is not his role to advise on or resolve domestic issues. Such assistance should be provided by the institution and Hassan should have been made aware of this at some sort of institutional induction. Institutions should also be aware that overseas postdocs working in any foreign country could have many cultural and personal issues to resolve which can easily lead to considerable anxiety. Institutional support in the early stages of a postdoc experience would therefore be invaluable. Having said all that, it would also be useful if mentors such as Dr. Rogers who hire overseas postdocs are made aware of and understand issues that may become problematic. It is probably going to be the case that unless Hassan's domestic issues are resolved quickly, he will be unable to make good progress in his research activities and this will lead to a certain amount of frustration on the part of Dr. Rogers. Therefore, in the short term at least, the relationship between Hassan and Dr. Rogers is still likely to be less than satisfactory.

What if the mentor–mentee relationship starts to go wrong; and finding a replacement mentor

The seriousness of a mentor–mentee relationship going wrong will often depend on what role the mentor is playing. If the mentor is the line manager and is responsible for providing funding of the research project, then it is particularly important that a working relationship be restored. For the ECR, it is important that you seek guidance from your local ECR committee or ECR administrative office, assuming that your institution has such resources. For the line manager, an obvious starting point would be to consult their Head of Department for guidance. If an acrimonious relationship cannot be resolved, then you have the option of leaving the project, although this may not be a desirable outcome. In rare instances, as in a recent case where an ECR questioned the reproducibility of date published by his mentor, the ECR's contract would be terminated as pressure forced him to resign a few days before a disciplinary hearing, at which he would have been dismissed (Reich 2011). Unfortunately, this example illustrates the vulnerability of ECR positions despite advances in employment practices.

If the mentor is not the line manager but is in the same institution, then a replacement mentor could be reallocated through the ECR committee or equivalent, or in the case of the Fellowship mentor via the ECR office. For a replacement probation mentor, it is likely that the Head of Department will be able to provide the solution. If you have a mentor/adviser outside the institution then it is very much your responsibility to find a replacement. If the problem is with the Society mentor, then the society or association concerned will have to suggest a replacement.

Summary

In almost all cases, you will require one or more mentors such as a research mentor and mentor/adviser, depending on what type of ECR you are. For example, a fellowship mentor is required to oversee the project in a similar way to the research mentor, although other types of mentor may be optional (see Table 3.1). The situation is further complicated as the topic of mentoring in general has been much neglected and the term mentor can be used in number of different contexts, and can refer to different roles. Because of the nature of the terminology and the growing independence of an ECR, it might be advantageous to use the term research mentor for your 'line manager'. It might be desirable if higher education institutions could create their own ECR mentoring plan, as the role of the ECR mentor/adviser could be developed in the same way that the PhD personal tutor role (as part of the supervisory team) has developed in the UK over the last few years.

Recommended/Further reading

Garvey, R., Stokes, P. and Megginson, D. (2009) *Coaching and mentoring: Theory and practice*. London: Sage.
This is the first authoritative text with a comprehensive overview and critical grounding in the key concepts, models and research studies in coaching and mentoring.

Chapter 4

Developing your writing and 'getting things written'

> I'm glad I did it, partly because it was worth doing, but mostly because I shall never have to do it again.
>
> (Mark Twain, c.1900)

Rather like Mark Twain's sentiments after finishing a piece of writing, one of the activities that many people, including experienced staff, find most difficult is the business of writing. This chapter argues that getting things written is an important element in an ECR's working life – but also that writing is a key part of a person's thinking and development process.

We look at different styles and approaches to writing that can be considered and perhaps adopted; then we selectively consider some of the published research and guidance on writing and try to distil the main points. We discuss the key question: what are the distinguishing features of skilled, productive writers?

There can be no single set of handy hints or infallible guidelines which apply to all writers and types of writing. So the main messages of this chapter are: writing is part of the thinking process; there is no one right way to write; draft and re-draft; and 'don't get it right, get it written'.

Classical models of writing and their dangers for ECRs

The traditional, popular model of writing was based on the idea that 'what you want to say and how you say it in words are two quite separate matters' (Thomas 1987). Others have called it the 'think and then write paradigm' (Moxley 1997: 6) i.e. you decide what you want to say, and then you write it down. Elbow (1973) is, like Moxley and Thomas, a critic of the so-called classic model, and he sums up the view as follows:

> In order to form a good style, the primary rule and condition is not to attempt to express ourselves in language before we thoroughly know our

meaning. When a man (sic) perfectly understands himself, appropriate diction will generally be at his command either in writing or speaking.

Thomas (1987: 95–98) analyses several ways in which a belief in this classical model can be harmful, or 'lead to trouble' as he puts it. First, belief in the model creates the expectation that writing should be easy if 'you know your stuff'. Then, when people find it difficult (as we all do) feelings of inadequacy and frustration set in. Second, the model leads to the implicit and incorrect belief that thorough knowledge will lead to clear, high quality writing. This is not always true and can again lead to negative feelings. Third, the expectation that writing is a linear process can lead to feelings of inadequacy and frustration as soon as the writer realises that it is in fact recursive or cyclical. Finally, the classic model goes something like: do all your reading, grasp your entire material, think it through, plan it out, then write. Writers who follow this would never get started.

In reality, thinking and writing interact. Thinking occurs during writing, *as* we write, not before it. Elbow (1973) described this model, the generative model, as involving two processes: growing and cooking. Writing various drafts and getting them on paper is growing; re-reading them, asking for comments from others and revising is part of the cooking process. Adopting and believing in this 'generative model' (Thomas 1987) will lead to several important attitudes and strategies:

- greater willingness to revise one's writing (drafting and re-drafting);
- a willingness to postpone the sequencing and planning of one's writing until one is into the writing process (it is easier to arrange and structure ideas and words once they are out there on paper, than in our heads);
- a habit of 'write first, edit later' (although this will not suit the working style of every writer, in our view);
- the attitude that extensive revisions to a piece of writing are a strength not a weakness;
- more willingness to ask for comment and feedback, and to take this on board;
- greater sensitivity to readers and their needs, prior experience and knowledge, and reasons for reading.

In fact, writing is a form of thinking – it is not something that follows thought but goes along in tandem with it (Wolcott 1990). Laurel Richardson (1990, 1998) often describes writing as a way of 'knowing', a method of *discovery* and analysis. Becker (1986: 17) puts it beautifully by saying: 'The first draft is for discovery, not for presentation'. This process of learning, discovery and analysis does not precede the writing process – it is part of it. Richardson tells of how she was taught, as many of us were, not to write until she knew what she wanted to say and she had organised and outlined her points. This model of writing has 'serious problems': it represents the social world as static and it 'ignores the role of writing as a dynamic, creative process' (Richardson 1998: 34). Most harmful, for new writers, is that the model undermines their confidence and acts as a block or obstacle in getting started on a piece of writing.

Planning, thinking and writing

The view that writing is a form of thinking does not rule out the need for planning. Plans are a starting point for writers. Although a few writers follow them meticulously most treat the plan as something to deviate from.

Here are some of the points made by three experienced authors who were interviewed by Jerry Wellington (all extracts taken from Wellington 2003, chapter 3):

> I usually pre-plan it, though on the occasions when I've just let it 'flow' it seems to have worked quite well. The surer I am of the theme the more natural it would be to let it flow, at least on first draft. I think I do a lot of thinking beforehand but invariably the act of writing is creative for me – some new links and strands pop up. I think I do structure my writing though the structure often gets revised.

> I put a lot of emphasis on pre-planning and particularly on structure, because the nature of what I write is argumentative. So I need the structure of the argument mapped out – and I work to this map. But quite often I don't actually, myself, understand fully what the argument is until I've done the first draft. So the first draft is a learning curve.

> I plan things visually, with a spidergram. I brainstorm ideas then try to connect them with a spidergram or a mind map. I find that, as I'm writing, the plan changes. If I write under sub-headings it's easier to move things. I can cut and paste, or move things to the bottom of the page if I don't know where to put them.

These comments show how the extent and style of planning seems to vary from one writer to another but all plan in some way. They also talk of learning through their writing, as opposed to writing activity occurring as a result of their learning. Learning and thinking come from writing rather than preceding it. This ties in with several studies reporting that writers see the act of writing as an aid to thinking (for example, Hartley 1992; Wason 1980)

Writing is difficult

Perhaps the main thing to remember about writing is that it is hard, even painful, work. Having extensive experience of writing does not make it easier, it simply makes the writer more confident. In discussing the question of 'what people need to know about writing in order to write in their jobs', Davies and Birbili (2000: 444) sum up by saying: 'We would suggest that the most important kind of conceptual knowledge about writing should be, in fact, that in order to be good it must be difficult.'

Interviews with different writers, many of them experienced and widely published, suggest that they all face barriers to writing – and the 'aids' they use to overcome so-called writers' block can be quite creative! (Again, these comments are taken from Wellington 2003, chapter 3):

> I get it all the time and I don't deal with it. I just stay there and plug away. I have to have total silence else I can't think. I do sometimes go and stand in the shower for 15 minutes or so and I find that can make me feel better.

> I don't know where to go next. Sometimes I just give up and do something else. Other times I go back to another chapter or a different sub-heading, or even my spidergram. Other times I just try to write my way through it, knowing that I'll probably delete most of it.

Different writers like to work at different times of the day, under different conditions and have different routines and avoidance strategies:

> I find procrastination to be a useless but common avoidance strategy. I write (and do most things) best in the morning and would regard 9 to 1 as being optimum writing time. I tend to leave routine chores (referencing, etc.) for late afternoon.

> I need silence, no noise at all. I write at the desk in my study, with the desk cleared of clutter. I write best in the morning between 8 and 1. A round-the-block or to-the-newsagents walk for 10 minutes helps enormously.

We suggest that many people, during writing, feel the need for incubation, for lying fallow, or for mulling things over during the business of writing something – especially during a long piece of work such as an extended paper or a book.

Getting started: when to stop reading and start writing

Starting a piece of writing is the hardest thing to do, except perhaps for finishing it (or at least knowing when to stop). Getting started on a piece of writing usually involves a kind of build-up to it: various authors have called this cranking-up, psyching up, mulling, organising, and so on (see Wolcott 1990: 13; Woods 1999). One of the ways of building up is to read widely (making notes on it, distilling thoughts, and jotting down your own ideas and viewpoints). The problem of course lies in knowing when to stop reading and to start writing. Initial reading is needed to help in the build-up process (cranking and psyching up) but one has to start writing before finishing reading – mainly because, in a sense, the reading can never stop. The two activities need to be balanced, with reading being on the heavier side of the see-saw initially and writing gradually taking over.

Ideally, the writer reaches a point where his or her own writing is just waiting to get out there, onto the page. But even then, most of us engage in all sorts of displacement activities: hoovering the hall carpet or walking the dog. Tidying up the hard disk on the computer or checking the e-mails as they come in can also be excellent distractions.

Time management for writing – or time creation . . .

One of the things that ECRs will not have is unlimited time to write.

Dorothea Brande (1983) in her classic book, first published in 1934, suggests that a beginning writer should start off by writing for a set period at the same time every day. Once this discipline becomes a habit she suggests that you can write at a different time each day, provided you always set yourself an exact time and keep to it. This advice may be too rigid and impossible to adhere to if one has a busy and unpredictable working day or a complicated home life (as most people now have, even if they did not in 1934). Brande tends to use a physical education (PE) analogy for writing, talking of exercise, training oneself to write, using unused muscles and the value of early morning writing. The PE analogy can be useful to a point (it can be helpful to think of keeping in trim, exercising our writing muscles and taking regular practice) but perhaps should not be over-stretched. Setting yourself a target word limit can help your goals feel more realistic – writing a book by Christmas might feel impossible, but writing 1,000 words a day is not so difficult, and might amount to the same thing.

One of the great dangers preventing us from finding or creating time to write is the tendency to wait for a big chunk of time to come along when we can 'really get down to it'. People convince themselves that productive writing will happen when they have a large block of uninterrupted time. This is one of the most common forms of procrastination: Boice (1997: 21) calls this the 'elusive search for large blocks of time. First colleagues wait for intersession breaks. Then sabbaticals. Then retirements.'

Haynes (2001: 12) suggests adopting simple routines for the beginning and end of each session. For example, one could begin with a 'freewriting' session of 4 or 5 minutes, just bashing out some words and sentences without pausing for correction, revision and certainly not editing. Haynes recounts that he likes to start a new writing session by making revisions to the text that he produced in the last one – a kind of warming up exercise. He also suggests the ploy of finishing a writing session before you have written everything you want to write, with the aim of making you look forward to the next session. Some writers, he claims, even end a session in the middle of a paragraph or even a sentence. Leaving yourself some notes about what should come in the next paragraph can serve a similar purpose – drawing you back into your flow of thought so that you don't have to recreate it from the beginning next time you start to write.

Abby Day (1996: 114–115) suggests that one should limit any writing session to a maximum of 2 hours. After that, one should take a break, perhaps have a walk or a coffee and come back to it another time feeling refreshed. This is also good health advice if working in front of a screen – most safety guidance suggests short breaks at frequent intervals away from the screen, standing up and looking at distant objects to rest the eyes and neck.

Different ploys, different times of day, different starting strategies will work for different people. The main general advice is to carve out some time to write when it suits your working and domestic day best, and your own preference for your 'best time'; and then try to write little and often, not hope for an entire day when you can work uninterrupted. This may never come and anyway, who can write productively for an entire day? Two or three hours, if you can find them, can yield as much good writing as a solid day that you look forward to with great expectations and then feel forced to write.

'Productive' writers

Hartley (1997) produced a useful summary based on his own research into what makes a productive writer in the discipline of psychology. His eight points can be transferred to writing in other areas, although point three looks a little dated now. His view was that 'productive writers' exhibit the following strategies. They:

1   Make a rough plan (which they don't necessarily stick to).
2   Complete sections one at a time (however, they don't always do them in order).
3   Use a word processor.
4   Find quiet conditions in which to write and if possible write in the same place or places.
5   Set goals and targets for themselves to achieve.
6   Write frequently, doing small sections at a time, rather than in long 'binge sessions'.
7   Get colleagues and friends to comment on their early drafts.
8   Often collaborate with long standing colleagues and trusted friends.

Haynes (2001: 11) offers an even shorter list of the 'qualities of productive writers'. From his experience as a commissioning editor, the productive writer:

* seeks advice
* shares drafts
* writes regularly (little and often).

These can all be applied to the situation of an early career researcher.

Skilled writers compared with unskilled

A large body of research has been published on the differences between 'good' and 'poor' writers. Flower and Hayes (1981), for example, concluded that good writers engage in 'global planning that incorporates rhetorical concerns such as audience, purpose and intention'. So-called 'poor writers' engage in local planning, focusing on surface features of their writing. These authors (Hayes and Flower 1986) also suggest that 'experts' revise more than novices, and attend more to global problems (e.g. re-sequencing, moving and re-writing large chunks of text). Skilled writers are better at diagnosing the problems in their texts and putting them right. Generally, however, writers find it harder to see problems in their own writing than they do in others' – hence the importance of a critical friend.

Grabe and Kaplan (1996: 240) give their own summary of the behaviours of good writers. Some characteristics of 'Good writers' are that they:

*   plan for a longer time and more elaborately;
*   review and re-assess their plans on a regular basis;
*   consider the reader's point of view when planning and composing;
*   revise in line with global goals and plans rather than merely editing small, local segments.

Grabe and Kaplan (1996: 118) also, rather cruelly, identify behaviours of 'less skilled writers'. Mainly, they begin to write 'much sooner' with less time taken for initial planning, producing less elaborate 'pre-writing notes'. They do not (or cannot) make major revisions or re-organisations of their content and they do not make use of overarching ideas across a text which could help with planning, composing and making the piece more coherent

Successful writing

Woods (1999) provides an excellent discussion of what he calls successful writing, for which one of his criteria is 'attention to detail'. He quotes the novelist David Lodge (see also Chapter 9) who describes how he learnt to 'use a few selected details, heightened by metaphor and simile, to evoke character or the sense of place' (quoted in Woods 1999: 13). The ability to connect or synthesize ideas is actually an aspect of creativity that sometimes shows itself in academic writing and research. It might be the ability to connect and interrelate one's own findings with existing research or theory; it might be a synthesis of ideas from two completely different domains of knowledge, e.g. using literature from a seemingly unrelated area; or it might be the application of a theory or model from one field to a totally new area. Syntheses or connections of this kind can be risky, and require a degree of self-confidence, but done well they can be illuminating and original.

In discussing the writing up of qualitative research, Woods (1999: 54–56) also talks of the importance of including 'other voices' in the text, besides that of the author. One of the objectives of social science research is to give people a voice or a platform, and this must be reflected in the written medium through which the research is made public. Giving people a voice, however, leads to some difficult choices. Every write-up is finite. Do you include lengthy statements or transcripts from one or two people, or many shorter points from a larger variety? (See Woods 1999: 56 for a discussion.) Woods urges qualitative researchers not to miss the humorous side of research, for example by including an ironic comment from an interviewee. All these approaches aim to give academic writing the life and character that will make it engaging and communicative to readers.

Another, very practical, issue when writing is knowing how many references to include when making a statement or a claim – for example, will one or two references do the job instead of a long list of perhaps six or seven, which can clutter the text somewhat? Deciding on this and thus avoiding 'over-referencing', is important for good writing and is another area where the help of a more experienced, critical friend or mentor can help greatly.

Structuring writing

The terms 'macrostyle' and 'microstyle' are sometimes used in looking at structure: the latter is concerned with style and structure at the level of words, sentences and paragraphs; while macrostyle is concerned with larger blocks and the overall structure and sequence. This distinction can be useful in thinking about writing and this section examines elements of both.

Macrostyle

There is considerable debate about how much structure authors should include in writing a report, thesis, book or article. The traditional scientific paper and most dissertations tend to follow the 'age-old' pattern of: Introduction, Methods/ Materials/Procedures, Results, Conclusions and Discussion. This tends to be the safe way of presenting a paper. However, over 40 years ago, the Nobel Prize winning scientist Sir Peter Medawar (1963, 1979) argued that although virtually all scientists write up their research as if it were a clean, linear, non-messy, carefully planned process, in reality the process is far more messy and cyclical; hence Medawar's famous accusation that the typical 'scientific paper is a fraud'. Despite this comment, it is worth noting that some scientific journals actually require a structure of this kind and state this in their instructions to authors – so although this template may be deemed a 'fraud' it is often a necessity for successful publication.

Now we go on to consider structure within a paper or chapter: headings and sub-headings; within chapters; paragraphing, connectives and sentence level.

Headings, sub-heading, sub-sub-headings . . .

Headings are valuable signposts in guiding a reader through a text and maintaining their interest or concentration. But it is always difficult to decide how many *levels* of heading to use. Headings need to be clear in a writer's mind, and then given a level in their manuscript (level A, level B and level C), each using a different font or typeface. For example:

Level A: **Main headings** (Initial capital, bold)
Level B: ***Sub-headings*** (Initial capital, bold italic)
Level C: *Sub-sub-headings* (Initial capital, italics)

If a writer goes 'below' level C this can be difficult. Writers, and readers, begin to flounder when they get past the sub-sub-level.

Chapter structure

Headings and sub-headings can help to structure an article or a chapter and break it down into digestible chunks. But there is also a useful rule, followed by many writers, which can help to give a chapter a feeling of coherence or tightness. This rule suggests that a chapter should have three (unequal in size) parts:

- A short introduction, explaining what the author is going to write about.
- The main body, presenting the substance of the chapter.
- A concluding section, rounding off the chapter.

This overall pattern works well for many writers, and readers, especially in a book chapter, conference paper or article. It is rather like the old adage associated with preaching: 'Tell them what you're going to say, then say it, and then tell them what you've just said.' For many types or genres of writing it works well and assists coherence. However, if overdone it can become tedious.

One other way of improving coherence is to write link sentences joining one paragraph to the next or linking chapters. For example, the last sentence (or paragraph) of a chapter could be a signal or an appetizer leading into the next. Beginning a new section or paragraph with a reference to the previous one is less effective – this means the reader who wants to focus on a specific section of your article or chapter has to look back in the text to make sense of it, so losing the flow of their reading.

Connecting phrases and sentences

One of the important devices in writing is the logical connective. Connectives are simply linking words and can be used to link ideas within a sentence, to link sentences or to link one paragraph to the next. Examples include: 'First', 'Second', 'Third', 'Finally'; also 'However', 'Nevertheless', 'Moreover', 'Interestingly', 'Furthermore', 'In addition', 'In conclusion', 'Thus', and so on.

Connectives can be valuable in maintaining a flow or a logical sequence in writing; but be warned – readers can suffer from an overdose if they are used too liberally, especially if the same one is used repeatedly. Ten 'howevers' on the same page can become wearing.

All the tactics and strategies summarised above have the same general aim: to improve clarity and communication. Table 4.1 gives a summary of four useful strategies which can be used in writing, whether it be an article, a book, a thesis or a conference paper.

Paragraphing

Different writers and different readers see paragraphs in different ways. If you give different readers a page of un-paragraphed prose and ask them to divide it into paragraphs, they are unlikely to break it down or categorise it in exactly the same way. A paragraph should ideally contain just one main theme or concept or category – but concepts come from people, and people vary (Henson 1999: 64). It takes practice, it is an art (Henson 1999: 66) and personal preferences will vary from one writer to another (and between editor and author sometimes).

Table 4.1 Four useful strategies in structuring writing

Strategy	Meaning	Examples
Signposting	Giving a map to the reader; outlining the structure and content of an article, book or chapter, i.e. structure statements	This chapter describes . . . The first section discusses . . . This paper is structured as follows . . .
Framing	Indicating beginnings and endings of sections, topics, chapters	Firstly, . . . Finally, . . . To begin with . . . This chapter ends with . . . To conclude . . .
Linking	Joining sentence to sentence, section to section, chapter to chapter . . .	It follows that . . . The next section goes on to . . . As we saw in the last chapter . . . Therefore . . .
Focusing	Highlighting, emphasising, reinforcing, key points	As mentioned earlier . . . The central issue is . . . Remember that . . . It must be stressed that . . .

Henson gives some useful tips on paragraphing (pages 37–38). He suggests that short paragraphs help the reader – the reader should be able to remember in one 'chunk' all the ideas contained in a paragraph. His rule of thumb is that half a side of double spaced typed text is enough for most readers to retain. Henson also suggests that whilst reading through what you've written, one should see if each paragraph follows from and advances upon the ideas in previous paragraphs. If not they should be re-ordered. This process, of course, is greatly helped by the cut-and-paste facility in word processing programs.

Getting it 'off your desk' and gradually exposing your writing

Reading your own work is important but is no substitute for having another eye on it. For an ECR the first person might perhaps be a 'critical friend' – this could be one of your peers or a close colleague. Then comes your mentor or supervisor – one of their roles and responsibilities is to read your written work and to help you develop it. Later (if possible) you might expose your writing to an 'outsider' e.g. an ECR from another department or someone in another university working in your field.

You, the writer, are not the best person to critique your own work. Your own tacit, implicit knowledge of what you wish to say makes it hard to identify the missing elements or steps in your own writing that can make it seem to other readers as though you have jumped to a conclusion without adequate premises. The Greek word 'ellipsis' (meaning 'cutting short') sums up these omissions neatly. Readers can spot a writer's ellipses more readily than writers can spot their own. Readers can also identify sentences that are clumsy or simply don't read well or 'sound right'. It is also easier to spot long-windedness or repetition in someone else's writing than in your own.

It is worth leaving your writing 'to stand' for a few weeks before re-reading it yourself, but the outside reader is essential too. Richardson (1990) talks of the value of 'getting early feedback' on your writing. This can be achieved by giving an 'in-progress' seminar or paper to fellow students, or in a departmental seminar, or using some other public forum such as a conference. Wolcott (1990: 46) suggests that reading your own words aloud to yourself can help, but even better a friendly colleague could read them to you so that you can listen and concentrate on 'what has actually reached paper – the experience you are creating for others, out of your own experience'. When the oral reader stumbles or 'gasps for air' (as Wolcott puts it) then it is time to 'get busy with the editing pencil'.

Editing, drafting and re-drafting

> I spent all morning putting a comma in, and the afternoon taking it out again.
> (attributed to Lord Byron, cited in Woodwark, 1992)

Most writers on writing seem to agree on one thing: Do not try to edit and write at the same time (Becker 1986; Henson 1999; Smedley 1993). Haynes (2001: 111) identifies two parts to the writing process: the compositional and the secretarial. In the first stage, writers should concentrate on getting words onto paper, generating text, trying to get the subject matter clear in their own minds and covering the ground. The secretarial stage involves sorting out the structure and layout, correcting things like spelling and punctuation and tinkering around with words and sentences. Haynes describes the first stage as 'writing for the writer', the second as 'writing for the reader'. This second stage is perhaps where the writer really needs to be aware of the intended audience; in the first stage, the writer can care far less about what anyone will think about it, and this slightly carefree attitude can encourage freer writing.

The act of editing can interfere with the activity of writing. Smedley (1993: 29) observes that 'when people first sit down to write, they begin a sentence and immediately take a dislike to the way it is worded and start again'. This is the editor interfering with the writer. Both are essential, but both should be kept in their places. 'The writer writes, the editor edits.' She suggests leaving the first draft for a day or a week and coming back to it with your editor's hat on this time. Editing involves seeing if it makes sense, feeling for how well it reads, asking if things could be put more neatly and succinctly and cutting unnecessary words. She argues for a number of drafts: 'Write without editing, then edit, then re-write without editing, then edit once again. When you exhaust your own critical eye as an editor, enlist the assistance of your spouse, your colleagues, your students, your trusted friends . . . and ask them to be brutal' (Smedley 1993: 30).

Becker (1986) believes that writers can 'start by writing almost anything, any kind of a rough draft, no matter how crude and confused, and make something good out of it'.

This could be called the pottery model of writing – start by getting a nice big dollop of clay onto the working area and then set about moulding and shaping. This model may not work for everyone though. Zinsser (1983: 97) talks of feeling that he writes rather like a bricklayer. His thoughts, written at the time by someone who had just discovered the value of the word processor, are worth seeing in full:

My particular hang-up as a writer is that I have to get every paragraph as nearly right as possible before I go on to the next one. I'm like a bricklayer. I build very slowly, not adding a new row until I feel that the foundation is solid enough to hold up the house. I'm the exact opposite of the writer who dashes off his entire first draft, not caring how sloppy it looks or how badly it's written. His only objective at this early stage is to let his creative motor run the full course at full speed; repairs can always be made later. I envy this writer and would like to have his metabolism. But I'm stuck with the one I've got.

Towards the final stages of editing and revising, a piece of advice given by Harry Wolcott (1990) seems very helpful. He tells of how the idea came to him when he was assembling a new wheelbarrow from a kit: 'Make sure all parts are properly in place before tightening.' Before you start tightening your writing, he argues:

> Take a look at how the whole thing is coming together. Do you have everything you need? And do you need everything you have?
>
> (Wolcott 1990: 48)

Watching every word and sentence

> I have made this letter longer than usual because I lacked the time to make it short.
>
> (Blasé Pascal, *Lettres Provinciales*, 1656–1657, no. 16)

A good old-fashioned guide by Bett (1952: 18) gives simple advice:

> the essence of style is the avoidance of (1) wind (2) obscurity. In your scientific writing be simple, accurate and interesting. Avoid like the plague 'as to whether' and 'having regard to', beloved of the drawers-up of legal documents. Avoid 'tired' words. Avoid 'slang'.

One of the old clichés, which is a tired one but does have some truth in it, is 'make every word work for a living'. Zinsser (1983: 98) offers one practical way of removing what he calls 'clutter'. He suggests reading the text and putting brackets round every word, phrase or sentence that 'was not doing some kind of work'. It may be a preposition that can be chopped out (as in 'free up', 'try out', 'start up', 'report back'); it may be an adverb that is already in the verb (as in 'shout loudly' or 'clench tightly'); it may be an unnecessary adjective (as in 'smooth marble'). Brackets could also be put round the qualifiers loved by academics and politicians, such as 'tend to', 'in a sense', 'so to speak', or 'in the present author's view' (the latter is also circumlocution). Entire sentences could be bracketed if they repeat something already said (unless it really needs re-inforcing) or add irrelevant detail (too much information perhaps). By bracketing the words or sentences as opposed to crossing them out, the reader/editor or writer can then see whether the text can really do without them – if so, then delete.

Incidentally, Zinsser (1983: 103) also emphasises the value of short sentences. He talks of how, in writing his own book:

> I divided all troublesome long sentences into two short sentences, or even three. It always gave me great pleasure. Not only is it the fastest way for a writer to get out of a quagmire that there seems no getting out of; I also like short sentences for their own sake. There's almost no more beautiful sight than a simple declarative sentence.

Haynes (2001: 93–96) gives excellent and witty advice on circumlocution. He identifies common examples such as 'at this moment in time' (meaning 'now'), 'until such time as' (meaning 'until'), 'is supportive of' (meaning 'supports') and 'is protective of' (meaning 'protects'). He suggests that two common causes of circumlocution are the use of euphemisms (e.g. 'going to meet their maker' instead of 'dying') and *pomposity*. There is no shortage of the latter in academic writing. Authors may attempt to impress their audience with a pompous tone and choice of words. They perhaps hope to appear knowledgeable and 'academic'. The end result is often the use of inappropriate and pretentious language. Haynes suggests that this may happen when authors 'feel superior to their audience', but also occurs when 'authors feel insecure either because they are short of material or they do not have a secure grasp of the subject' (Haynes 2001: 94). It is certainly something to beware of, either as a reader or a writer. Every sentence, in a book, chapter, conference presentation or article should make sense. [3,4]

Scenario 4.1 – Finding time to write

Nikki had been delighted to get a postdoctoral position in the Department of Sociological Studies at her local university, and was finding her work on a funded project about teenage drug use challenging and fulfilling. The lead researcher on the project was ambitious for their study, aiming to get their findings into top-rated journals, and often telling Nikki that there was no point in going for 'easy' journals, even though a publication there might move more quickly through the review process and get into print within a year. While Nikki could see the point of that argument, she would have welcomed the opportunity to gain a publication more quickly, knowing that this would be valuable for her own future career. She resolved repeatedly to concentrate instead on publishing from her own recent doctoral studies, but finding time to do this was really difficult, especially as it felt as though there was always more to be done on the drug project – which, after all, paid her wages. Nikki felt as though she needed a clear block of time for her writing – having an hour here and there wasn't enough to switch her mind back from the current study to her PhD work. The only option was to use her weekends for writing, but she was often tired from the week's work, so progress was slow and unsatisfactory – and her boyfriend was beginning to complain that he never saw her. Against these pressures, her thesis continued to languish in the pile beside her desk, and Nikki began to doubt whether her research would ever reach publication.

The short selection of comments from members of our focus group relates to, and helps to illustrate, some of the issues raised in the above scenario:

Personal issues

> There is always something else you could be doing . . . start another experiment, do another control . . .

> When you're a researcher on someone else's project there is always pressure to crack on, get back to the lab. And collect more data, rather than writing.

> Your research can sometimes get in the way of publishing what you want to publish. On top of my research job I then need to create time for writing and publishing.

> For me it's just the time it takes . . . which is hard to justify if you're not certain of the outcome. In a tenured post it's easier than for a researcher. There's only so much time a line manager will allow you. You can't write if you've only got an hour here or there.

Striving for perfection . . . and not knowing when to stop . . . is a problem for many of us, as this quotation sums up:

> I'm never happy with my writing; I always want to do more and more. It's never perfect but I want to make it perfect . . .

Scenario 4.2 – Writing with a critical friend

As an early career researcher in Materials Science, Chris knew well the importance of publishing, but felt that he had always struggled with academic writing, feeling that it came more easily to other people but doubting his own abilities. He was fortunate in having a sympathetic boss, who was himself a very productive and prolific writer, and seemed to have the knack of going straight to the point of what was wrong with a draft – often a lack of structure, or an attempt to cover too much ground in trying to turn a large-scale study into a 6,000 word article. As his mentor offered guidance, Chris began to spot the strategies in his recommendations and to try and plan these into his own writing, so gradually the earliest drafts became more proficient and his skills at revising his own writing improved. He knew he was fortunate in having a 'critical friend' in his boss: other postdocs in the department weren't so lucky and had to ask friends or partners to provide feedback for them, which could be fraught with relationship difficulties!

Over the 3 years of his postdoc, the comments on Chris's draft articles became less extensive, and while he sometimes worried that his boss was simply losing patience with looking at drafts, the positive comments he started to receive from reviewers on submitting his articles reassured Chris that his writing was indeed improving. The prospect of an academic career was starting to look more realistic and more enjoyable than he could have hoped 3 years earlier.

The short selection of comments from members of our focus group relates to, and helps to illustrate, some of the issues raised in the above scenario. We asked the ECRs in the focus group: whom do you go to for help and guidance?

Personal issues

My line manager or I just go to the most relevant person in the department.

I go to my husband for feedback before I go to my supervisor. I like to get an outsider's perspective.

My supervisor is very good at putting a 'selling point' onto an article, putting in punchy sentences, adding spin to it. He's not interested in seeing the first draft.

But the role of the supervisor can be contentious . . .

Sometimes supervisors have your interests in mind . . . but sometimes they don't. They might want you to keep going with your writing towards the 'big' journals . . . whereas you might want to take incremental steps on the publishing ladder. There can be a big difference of opinion about what to publish and where.

And finally . . . writing with a view to 'getting published' . . .

In the next chapter we explore publishing and some of the perceived obstacles to publishing. We asked our focus group two sets of questions about publishing: first, why write and publish, and what motivates you to write?; second, what puts you off? To lead into that chapter we present some of the comments of focus group members on those questions. The issues raised are expressed here and explored in Chapter 5:

Personal issues

Having work published can be a very positive experience with words and terms such as 'accolade', 'peer recognition', 'validation' and 'getting known' being used.

From a career perspective, it's very useful to present at conferences, to get feedback and to produce conference papers from it . . . and these can lead to full-blown articles.

To try to put your work out there: as an ECR if you want to become an academic you need to be known by others in your field. It's a way of being noticed.

It's a validation of the work you've done.

It shows that you can see a project through from beginning to end . . . through to publication.

On the other hand there are problems:

There is a steep curve between your first draft and when you send it off.

If you have worked together as a group, sometimes the sheer effort of sitting down together to work out the order of the authors can put you off!

Time lag is a problem with publication when you're on a short term contract and looking for your next job.

Finally, one comment is reminiscent of the Mark Twain quote at the start of this chapter:

I recently wrote something for a journal and I was asked to revise it five times . . . by which point I couldn't care if it got published or not. I only wanted it published so that I never had to see it again.

Summary

We hope that this chapter has offered some guidance, re-assurance and insight for those embarking on the challenging task of 'getting it written'. The intention of the chapter is to admit that writing is indeed 'hard work' but our aim is to encourage you to write and (as in the next chapter) to publish. For many ECRs the problem is often a question of what to leave out from a mass of results and data, rather than not having enough to write about and discuss – this is once again where a mentor or a critical friend can come in.

Our parting messages are: the writing process is a complex one; it is in some senses a struggle for many people; reflecting on our own writing processes is a valuable activity; it is comforting to share these reflections with peers; it is important to expose your writing to others – peers, critical friends and your mentor – as soon as possible ; there is a range of styles and approaches to planning and composing – but there is no one right way of writing.

Recommended/Further reading

Many of the references used in this chapter offer valuable advice on writing. Two classics from the past for social scientists and scientists respectively are Becker and Medawar.

Becker, H. (1986) *Writing for social scientists: How to start and finish your thesis, book or article*. Chicago, IL: University of Chicago Press.
Medawar, P. (1979) *Advice to a young scientist*. New York: Harper and Row.

Wolcott and Woods provide excellent advice for 'qualitative' researchers who wish to present their work in an engaging and scholarly way.
Wolcott, H. (1990) *Writing up qualitative research*. Newbury Park, CA: Sage.
Woods, P. (1999) *Successful writing for qualitative researchers*. London: Routledge.

Whitesides offers specific advice for scientists and engineers in preparing papers based on empirical research.
Whitesides, G. (2004) Whitesides' group: writing a paper. *Advanced Materials*, 16(15): 1375–1377.

Chapter 5

Getting published

One of the pressures on, and responsibilities of, ECRs is to publish. But this is easier said than done. This chapter considers the reasons why ECRs could and should make an effort to disseminate their work. It also considers the converse: what factors act as barriers in putting people off or preventing publication? We then move on to the 'what' and how of publishing by looking at types of publication and strategies for getting your work published in journals, as book chapters or even as a book.

Why publish?

One of the first things to discuss, with both your peers and your mentor, is the question: why publish? This is the starting point because it will determine not only which parts of your work you might aim to disseminate more widely but also *which targets* you should aim for (e.g. journal or book? Which types of journal? Book chapters?) and whom you should work with in achieving these goals.

A whole host of reasons is given in answering this question. Some involve intrinsic rewards, some extrinsic. Some are to do with outside pressures and accountability. Some relate to the satisfaction of writing and its value in aiding thinking.

Wellington (2003) discusses seminars on publishing that he has been running for new lecturers for a number of years which always begin with the question of: what are your motives for wanting to publish? The responses are many and varied (several have been recorded in more detail in Wellington 2003: 2–11). Quite commonly, the motivations are extrinsic: to improve my CV, to contribute to research assessment exercises, to get a steady job, to gain promotion, to join the research community, to earn respect and credibility, to enhance my standing, to become known and so on. But equally commonly, the motivation for publishing is more an intrinsic one: to clarify my own thinking, to share my ideas more widely, personal satisfaction, contributing to change and improvement, to make a difference, to set up a dialogue, and so on.

So – why publish? The main answer we would give to ECRs, though it might sound elitist and hard-nosed, is that it is quite simply 'part of the job'. Publishing comes with the territory – it is not some sort of hobby or sideline that some people somehow find time for. If one does 'not have the time', then (as the Union leaders used to say) a 'full and frank exchange' with the head of department is needed to create it. Time needs to be given to people to write, assuming that it is part of the job. Time is a necessary (though often not a sufficient) condition for writing and publishing to take place. Time for writing has to be 'managed', by both managers and individuals. However, every ECR's reasons and motives to publish are many and varied; this needs to be borne in mind when working out one's own publications strategy.

Incidentally, Whitesides, a Harvard science professor, is clear and direct on this issue:

> If your research does not generate papers, it might just as well not have been done. 'Interesting and unpublished' is equivalent to 'non-existent'.
>
> (Whitesides 2004: 1375)

Why not publish . . . or what puts people off?

Before looking at tactics and strategy i.e. the how of publishing, we need to consider the other side of the coin: the factors that prevent people from publishing or even attempting to do so. Responses are again many and varied (Wellington 2003: 6–7) but include such feelings as: lack of self-belief, fear of criticism or rejection, not knowing where to begin, wondering 'am I good enough', not having a track record, lack of time and energy, not knowing the right targets; fear of being judged; not knowing how to respond to criticism; fear of exposure, vulnerability, putting one's head 'above the parapet', and so on (some of the more general barriers to writing itself are discussed in Chapter 4). [5]

The impostor syndrome

One of the reasons people give for not publishing is what Brookfield (1995: 229) calls the 'impostor syndrome'. He discusses it in the context of teaching but it is paralleled in writing. It is the feeling of 'am I teaching (writing) this under false pretences?' Do I really know what I'm talking about? The syndrome feeds on lack of confidence; fear of being 'found out' or of not being as competent as others might think we are; feelings of inadequacy, of not being worthy; fears of being revealed as a fraud; possession of an inferiority complex. Brookfield calls it one of the dangers of critically reflecting on our own practice.

At its worst, the so-called syndrome can be inhibiting and create feelings of impotence and inferiority. This alone can be enough to stop people from exposing their writing. But, if brought into the open and shared, it can have a positive effect. It can lead to (or indeed is a feature of) a sense of humility, of recognising one's own limitations. Not only that, think of the opposite to the impostor syndrome: conceit, a superiority complex, super-confident assertion, lack of reflection, incaution, the kind of brash over-confidence that some people in academic and political life seem to have been imbued with i.e. the ability to speak confidently and sound knowledgeable on any subject, even if they know nothing about it. No thank-you.

Factors that help people to publish

All of the above motivating *and* de-motivating factors are important in considering how to proceed and specifically, how to work with your mentor. For example, if your aim is to gain a job or promotion within academia, then you should be consulting your mentor about which targets for publications – probably academic journals – are most appropriate. On the other hand, if your work relates to a particular profession then the motivation for publishing and the most productive 'outlet' for it will be different. When we consider 'de-motivating' factors then the role of the mentor in guiding and assisting is equally important. If an ECR has no track record (a likely position) and lacks confidence or does not know where to begin, then the collaboration and direct help of mentor and colleagues is essential. ECRs may wish to co-author with their mentor and this can often be the best way to get started. If someone wishes to go it alone, then the advice from mentor and colleagues on content, critical reading and guidance on potential journal target or book publisher is vital. There are commonly senior staff in the department, whom your mentor can help you liaise with, who may be editors of major journals, or on editorial boards or (equally likely) will have good contacts with commissioning editors for book publishers.

Our advice is to use all the networks and contacts that you can find when it comes to publishing and finding a 'target' for your work. Your mentor and other colleagues can play a central part in this as a facilitator, adviser, guide, or co-author – or all of these roles.

In short, making a concerted effort to remove some of the barriers above is the first stage in writing for publication. Given the necessary condition of having time to write, other factors can be a major catalyst: the presence of encouraging, supportive colleagues; the assistance of a critical friend or friends; having one's confidence boosted; and finally, receiving concrete guidelines and advice on writing and publishing. The aim of the rest of this chapter is to present some of these guidelines (gleaned from various sources) and thus to look at concrete suggestions for the 'what' and the 'how' of getting published, with the above fears and apprehensions in mind.

What types of publication should you aim for?

There is a range of possibilities for disseminating and presenting work in progress or work completed: some will involve spoken presentations, probably using visual aids; some will involve writing for conference proceedings, journals or book publishers; dissemination may involve a combination of spoken and written forms. Table 5.1 gives a summary of the main types of publication that could emerge from a research study.

Table 5.1 Main types of research publication (adapted from Wellington and Szczerbinski 2007)

Articles ('papers') in peer-reviewed journals	With respect to their content, papers can be divided into: *Primary literature:* reports of new, previously unpublished data. *Narrative literature reviews:* critical summaries of a current state of knowledge on a given topic. *Quantitative literature reviews/meta-analyses:* 'pulling together' and statistical reanalysis of results of all (quantitative) studies on one particular topic, in order to draw a general conclusion about their outcome.
Books	With respect to authorship and editorial process, academic books may be divided into: *Scholarly monographs:* books addressing a single topic, written by one or few authors. *Edited books:* books where each chapter is written by different authors. Chapters are revised by editors, who take responsibility for overall consistency, coherence and cohesion. They usually (though not exclusively) address a single topic from a range of perspectives.
Presentations at conferences (organised by learned societies or professional organisations)	Different forms are possible: *Oral presentations:* oral accounts (typically using visual aids) of research in front of the peer audience. *Posters:* a 'single page' summary of research, presented during 'poster sessions' that are part of most conferences, often with the opportunity to stand by your poster and answer questions. *Conference proceedings:* printed summaries of research presented during conferences. May be very brief (abstracts) or more substantial (resembling research papers).
Commissioned reports	The commissioning body may be the government, a charity, a quango, a commercial company, etc.
Other	*Technical reports:* Typically prepared for internal distribution (e.g. for a sponsor of the research project). *Working papers:* reports of work in progress, ahead of more formal peer-reviewed publication. They are often made available online. *Blogs:* blogs as a means of disseminating research findings have been increasingly adopted (e.g. by some scientists researching online communities).

The first stage for many ECRs will be to present their work internally, for example at departmental seminars or an internally organised conference. Presenting to your peers can be a valuable experience for both presenter and audience. Another forum is the workshop or presentation session at a research association conference. A third audience for certain disciplines is fellow practitioners, certainly for the researching professional. All or any of these modes of presentation can be used either to present 'work in progress' or 'work completed'.

One of the difficult issues for ECRs will be the decision on **when to publish.** Shortly we consider the business of 'turning' a dissertation into a publication but in many disciplines (certainly in science and engineering) students are encouraged, very usefully in many cases, to write papers during their doctoral programme. In deciding on when to publish, the questions to address with your supervisor and/or mentor are: should I publish the set of experiments I am working on, or the theory that is developing, now or should I wait? More instrumentally, can I design experiments to make sure that they are publishable? (the latter is discussed helpfully in Whitesides 2004).

Converting your thesis to a 'publication'

Whether they have published already or not, for many ECRs, the last thing they feel like doing after completing a doctorate is to return to their thesis and start to 'chop it up' and 'mould' it into some other form or forms. But this is exactly what is often required. Perhaps the best tactic is to ignore it for several weeks, putting some time and distance between you and it, and then to return to it with the explicit aim of disseminating your work and 'getting published'.

You will need to think about the benefits and implications of publishing as a sole author, or in collaboration with someone else – most often your supervisor or mentor. In the sciences, where doctoral work is often carried out as part of a research team, there is a strong expectation that your supervisor and other researchers will be co-authors, listed in order of their contribution to the study – so in the case of your doctoral work, it is likely that your name should come first. In the arts and humanities, sole-authored publications are still the norm, and later in your career you may find that a paper with only your name on it is more valuable for promotion, research assessment, and so on, than one co-authored with your supervisor. You should ask more experienced colleagues for their views on this, and follow the precedents of your department or discipline. If you are involved in co-writing, try to ensure that this is a genuinely collaborative process, sharing ideas at every stage of the writing, and forming a new intellectual relationship with your mentor that goes beyond their checking and correction of your draft writing. Whatever your decision about naming authors, never try to be completely independent in your first attempts at publication: in most departments there is a wealth of advice, experience and contacts to draw upon, and established colleagues will often be happy to read and discuss your writing, and so help you to avoid the pitfalls that they will almost certainly have encountered when they made their own first forays into print.

The first task is to set some goals. The thesis may contain different papers for different audiences: for example, there may be an important article to be written from the thesis on the methodology or even the specific methods used. This might be targeted (see later) on one journal. Another article might be written on the findings and their implications for practice – this might be geared at a more 'professional' journal, aimed at practitioners such as engineers, health professionals, teachers or lecturers. Third, within the thesis there might be an article that can contribute to thinking and theory within an area; and finally, between the two poles of practice and theory, there might be important messages for policy makers and planners, and this might be targeted at a refereed journal on policy or a more 'professional' journal for policy makers. Alternatively, if your thesis was an interdisciplinary one, you might want to target particular themes or findings at journals in related disciplines, and so contribute to connecting research across several different readerships. In making decisions about the numbers of papers to write, think about how to disseminate your research as widely as possible, without 'over-working' it – it is too early in your career to become known as someone who publishes the same thing repeatedly! (A 'salami slicer'.)

If the goal is to be a book, then it might contain a combination of all the above. However, commercial book publishers will want a clear statement of the potential market for the book and this is discussed shortly.

Going for journal articles

Books are written for markets – journal articles are written for peers. Different rules of engagement apply. We do not have the space in this book to explore fully the intricacies of writing, refereeing and editing journals (for a fuller account, see Wellington 2003, chapter 4). All we can do here is sum up some of the key tips for new writers (Table 5.2) and indicate some of the things 'not to do' (Table 5.3).

Perhaps the main point is that we suggest that you should have a clear target journal in mind *before* you write your article, not after. This means that your first job is to become aware of all the possible journals in your field that are potential targets. You will then need to consider the status of the possible journals and their so-called 'impact factor' (see the Scenario at the end of the Chapter).

You should also be aware of the following: there will be considerable time lags between submission and receiving referees' comments – and between acceptance and actual appearance in print (in the region of 2 years in some cases); peer review can be difficult to accept, but you should view it positively i.e. as 'free feedback' and a way of making your article better; do expect to have to make at least some revisions to your first submission; you may be rejected by one journal – if so, then improve your first version and send it to another journal as soon as possible. Be sure to learn from and respond to the feedback – in a small field of research, your work could well go back to the same expert reviewers, who won't be impressed to read it in unchanged form a second time!

Table 5.2 Writing for journals: Tips for improving acceptance chances

- Select a journal and familiarise yourself with it i.e. select your target journal carefully and tailor your manuscript to suit it and its intended audience. This can be done in the following specific ways:
  - Observe how past authors have structured their writing.
  - Check journal style and past practice on headings and sub-headings.
  - Look for recurring topics, debates and themes in the target journal.
  - Decide on the type of journal and who it is for i.e. wide ranging or specialist? Professional or academic? Refereed or non-refereed?
  - Read a good number of back issues and shape your article accordingly.
  - Look for traits / characteristics in a journal and attempt to 'model' them.
Then in your own written submission . . .
- Try to make a unique contribution, however small – and to make this clear to the reader in your abstract and conclusions.
- Try to write clearly and coherently.
- Have a clear 'argument' or thesis running through it.
- Include a 'so what?' section.
- Keep to the word length.
- *Follow the journal's guidelines to authors, especially on citation style and referencing.*
- Ask a critical friend to read it before sending it off.

The main message is that you should not be discouraged by reviews that say you need to make changes (this is to be expected, not feared) – make the changes and that journal will often publish the revised version. The best tactic in making changes is to consider each of the reviewers' comments in turn and respond to it, indicating to the editor in a letter accompanying your re-submission exactly what you have done in each case. Keep the tone professional here, despite temptations that may occur to be either defensive or even sarcastic (for example, with reviewers who unfortunately may have shown sarcasm to you or seem not to have really read your paper!). You do not need to capitulate

Table 5.3 Writing for journals: common mistakes

Lack of familiarity with the journal, its style and its readership.
Wrong style, wrong formatting, etc.
Wrong length.
Poor presentation, e.g. grammatical errors, typos.
No substance – 'much ado about nothing'.
Un-readability, i.e. writing is unclear, turgid, or does not make sense.
Manuscript not checked and proof-read.

on every point but you will need an explanation of your responses which will satisfy the editor.

Writing for publication requires you to re-think your audience: over the past few years, you will have become accustomed to writing for your supervisor, and later for your examiners – now your work is going out to a wider readership, you need to think about engaging them and telling them something new, rather than (quite so much) defending and justifying your ideas. The purpose of a literature review, for instance, shifts slightly: rather than establishing your academic credentials by proving to your PhD examiners that you've read everything of relevance in your field, the first pages of an article now need to locate your research for your new, unfamiliar readers. Don't include long lists of references that simply demand credit for effort; instead think about the salient points within the literature, and identify the questions and topics on which your article will build. Bear in mind that if you're writing for a specialist journal a lot of your readers will know this literature too, so your own original contribution should be the main focus of the article. For a general, professional publication, the challenge in changing your author voice might be in making your research more accessible, and highlighting its interesting applications rather than going into laborious details on theory and methods. Once again, careful perusal of previous articles in your target publication will help you to judge the right tone for your readership.

Finally, there is one definite *Don't* with journal articles. It is now an accepted ethical code in most fields (written in some cases, tacit in others) that authors should never submit to more than one journal concurrently i.e. submit in series, not parallel, even though this takes time.

The book?

Commercial publishers will not publish books that people are unlikely to buy. For example, no commercial book publisher will ever accept a traditional thesis exactly as it stands and 'convert' it straight into a book. (See Wellington 2003, chapter 5, for evidence to support this trend.) The conversion is your job – but, as mentioned above, the task of converting a thesis into a book is no small one. It involves radical changes to the content, including much chopping down. It will need a new title, agreeable to the publisher. The audience and therefore the style of writing will be different. In short, it requires severe editing, extensive re-writing and certainly a large element of 're-packaging' or re-moulding.

No one should ever write a book before seeking and finding a publisher, having one's proposal scrutinised and advised upon, and then receiving a contract safely in hand. Book proposals require considerable thought partly because, unlike theses, books have to be sold, meaning that somebody must want to buy them. Usually, a proposal will consist of a synopsis of the book and one or two sample chapters. But what else should a typical proposal contain? There is a fair measure of agreement amongst different publishers on the sections that should be covered in a good book proposal. These are summarised in Table 5.4.

Table 5.4 The key elements in a book proposal

The provisional title of the book.

Its proposed contents: what will the book be about?

A synopsis.

The market, the intended readership: who is going to buy it?

The competition: how will it compare with, compete with or complement existing books?

Who is the author or authors? (Include a short biography.)

The timescale and writing plan: when will the script be ready?

Production requirements: how long will it be (the extent); how many tables, illustrations etc. will it contain?

Sample material: one, or at most two, draft chapters.

Potential referees for this proposal.

If anyone would like full details and further insight, based on interviews with publishers, the business of writing a book proposal and publishers' criteria for acceptance are discussed at length in Wellington (2003: 81–95). In addition, most commercial publishers provide their own guidelines and pro-forma and a search of their websites can yield much useful advice (see Further Reading at the end of this chapter).

Our own experience with publishers and their commissioning editors is that they are extremely helpful and will often support a good idea even if it will not result in the sale of tens of thousands of books. However, one point is worth bearing in mind from a career point of view: authors who intend to forge a career in 'academia' will be subject to research assessment exercises – hence, they need to be conscious of steering the right course between audience appeal and scholarly substance. A book with popular appeal may not always carry the same kudos as an article in a high status journal but it can certainly increase the impact of one's work and the breadth of the readership.

And finally – what did publishers ever do for us (authors)?

Some ECRs might well be tempted to go it alone in seeking to make their ideas or data public and disseminate their hard-worked-for research. This is increasingly possible given the World Wide Web and the Internet as a platform for expressing and spreading ideas and findings. Indeed, some editorial boards have actually divorced themselves from commercial publishers who may be overcharging for subscriptions or simply getting in the way, and set up their own, autonomous e-journals. Prior to the advent of e-publishing the opportunities for authors to go their own way were limited to either engaging in self-publishing or kitchen table publishing – or in some cases, vanity publishing by which a publisher is paid to take on work, produce it and disseminate it.

So, it is worth stopping to consider what contribution publishers of books or journals make to the overall furtherance of publication and scholarship. First, they can offer improved presentation of one's work – in terms of what is still called 'typesetting': attractive covers, binding and generally improved appearance and layout. Second, journals in particular offer *archiving to your writing* i.e. if your article appears in a journal it becomes part of an archive, perhaps stretching back a long way. You become part of a series, with a track record and a history. Third, the traditional publication process (book or journal) offers improved content and enhanced quality. A journal effectively gives you free feedback (even if it is painful) on your writing. It also provides proof reading, editing and copy-editing. Fourth, improved publicity and marketing: publishers have links and networks with the academic community, librarians, library suppliers, book-shops and booksellers. How many 'kitchen table' authors and publishers could claim the same links? Publishers' links, of course, provide far better distribution and therefore dissemination of your work. Next, traditional publishing offers enhanced status to the author, which vanity, self or kitchen table publishing could not. The fact that your writing has been through an editorial and review process gives it some mark of quality and authority. Finally, commercial publishers do offer some degree of protection of an author's material from potential offenders. For example, the publisher will observe and enforce copyright law and is usually able to take legal action if work is pirated or plagiarised.

In summary, publishers can provide improved presentation, content, dissemi-nation and marketing; publishing can enhance kudos, and will protect and archive your material. For all these reasons, the traditional channels of publication bestow huge advantages. They do carry a cost, in terms of energy and time and being subjected to a review process that may be lengthy, painful and in some cases allegedly less than fair – but it is worth it.

Scenario 5.1 – How do you know which journal to send your manuscript to?

Francis had managed to publish one piece of work already with the help of his PhD supervisor, Dr. Summers, who advised him of how to prepare the manuscript and to which journal it should be sent. Indeed, it was a big moment for Francis to see his name in print and it made all the back-breaking research for the early part of the PhD now seem very worthwhile. Although Francis had now moved on to his ECR position overseas, he realised that the latter part of the PhD, which in some ways had generated some more interesting data, had still not been written up for a paper. This was something he was determined to do as soon as he could find the time, but the problem in preparing the manuscript was that he didn't really know how good the data were in making a judgement to aim for the highest impact factor journal. If he decided to aim for a very high impact factor journal, it might get rejected and there was always the chance that someone else might beat him to publish similar data. On the other hand, if he chose a journal with too low an impact factor, it would debase the value of his research and would not be as impressive for his CV. So, what was he to do?

Francis decided that he really must consult Dr. Summers as he would naturally be a co-author anyway. Dr. Summers quickly responded to his message as he was really excited about Francis's data and considered them particularly exciting in the light of some new developments. So it was decided to submit to a reasonably prestigious journal. Unfortunately, this journal did not wish to publish as their two reviewers were extremely critical of the work and were demanding further data to provide confirmation of findings. Of course, Francis was bitterly disappointed but Dr. Summers held his nerve and was quite confident of the importance of Francis's data. He suggested to Francis that they submit to a similar journal which had a slightly higher impact factor. Much to the surprise of Francis, this journal was willing to accept the manuscript subject to some minor modifications. This was a great outcome for Francis and would certainly go some way in promoting his career.

Summary

This chapter has explored the reasons for publishing, the benefits that publishers can provide and some of the factors that put people off. We have also looked at categories for potential publication and some of the tactics when aiming for a journal article or book.

Our suggestion in this chapter is that when it comes to publishing, go for it. The first place to look is often your dissertation. For many established authors, their first academic book or journal article was a by-product of their Masters or Doctoral thesis; many theses have the potential to be transformed into a book, a book chapter or an article or more. The article or book is unlikely to have the extensive data presentation, tables of results, comprehensive literature review, methodology discussion, terms of conditionality, appendices and plethora of references that would be expected in a doctoral thesis – but its central themes, its original contribution to knowledge and its innovative ideas and discussion are all likely to interest a book publisher or a journal editor.

Disseminating your ideas and sharing work and data at conferences, in papers and journal articles, and books or book chapters can all play a part in becoming part of a research and teaching community. It is part of the job and can be one of the most enjoyable parts.

Recommended/Further reading/Links

Websites

Publishers' websites with good guidance for ECR writers include Taylor and Francis, who offer advice on writing a journal article, and Ashgate, who give a detailed account of how (and whether) to turn your thesis into a book:

http://journalauthors.tandf.co.uk/preparation/writing.asp
http://www.ashgate.com/Default.aspx?page=1671

Books

Wellington, J. (2003) *Getting published*. London: Routledge.
Offers general advice and guidance on the 'why, what and how' of publishing for journals and book publishers.

Whitesides, G. (2004) Whitesides' Group: writing a paper. *Advanced Materials*, 16(15): 1375–1377.
Provides useful guidance, mainly for scientists and engineers, on developing papers for publication starting from what Whitesides calls 'outlines'.

Video

Whitesides has also produced a very personal and engaging video account on 'Publishing your research' available at:

http://pubs.acs.org/page/publish-research/episode-1.html

Chapter 6

Applying for research funding

Your research mentor may have suggested it, your institution may encourage it, but how and why would you want to apply for research funding? Preparing, writing and winning (or not!) a research grant is a serious undertaking, that requires a lot more than identifying a research topic. There are elements in research grant applications that you may not have thought of before – e.g. who will fund the idea, who will benefit academically, economically or socially from the research, how much does it cost? After writing and submitting the grant proposal it also doesn't stop there: your peers judge it, you may have an interview as part of the selection process, and if successful, you then have to manage and deliver the research. However, obtaining funding can accelerate your research and career prospects by enabling you to channel your efforts, buy you resources, and can increase your academic reputation.

A key part of any research career is the process of applying for funding to conduct research. There are many different types of funding bodies such as government agencies and charities, which provide different types of resources to support research. The specific funding body dictates the type, timing and level of funding available and also the area of research they are willing to support (Table 6.1). The funding bodies also manage the eligibility criteria and selection process, and their decision is final. As an ECR you may take the opportunity to apply for research funding but should you or can you do this, and where do you start?

In essence a research grant is 'funding for work that is intended to meet the proposer's need' (Grove 2004). As an ECR you may get involved in applying for research funding as either a lead investigator (i.e. principal investigator [PI]) or as part of a team of researchers (co-investigator [Co-I] or researcher co-investigator). Deciding which strategy to take can be dependent on simple factors such as eligibility criteria of the relevant funding body or even the terms and conditions of your employment contract. For example, the UK Engineering and Physical Sciences Research Council allows ECRs on fixed term contracts to be identified as a researcher co-investigator (rather than PI or Co-I), if they have made a substantial contribution to the development of the application, with the

Table 6.1 Examples of types of fellowships available to ECRs within the UK

Funding Body	Name or type of scheme
Arts and Humanities Research Council (AHRC) www.ahrc.ac.uk	• Fellowships (Early Career Route)
British Academy www.britac.ac.uk	• Postdoctoral Fellowships
Economic and Social Research Council (ESRC) www.esrc.ac.uk	• Placement Fellowships • Future Leaders
Engineering and Physical Sciences Research Council (EPSRC) www.epsrc.ac.uk	• Research Fellowships • First Grant Scheme
Royal Academy of Engineering www.raeng.org.uk	• Research Fellowships
Toshiba http://www.toshiba-europe.com/eur/fellowship/	• Fellowship Programme
Daphne Jackson Foundation www.daphnejackson.org	• Fellowship
CERN – European Organization for Nuclear Research www.cern.ch	• Junior fellowship programme
European Space Agency www.esa.int	• Postdoctoral research fellowships
Natural Environment Research Council (NERC) www.nerc.ac.uk	• Postdoctoral Research Fellowship • Advanced Research Fellowships
Biotechnology and Biological Sciences Research Council (BBSRC) www.bbsrc.ac.uk	• David Phillips Fellowships • New Investigator Scheme • Institute Career Path Fellowships
Medical Research Council (MRC) www.mrc.ac.uk	• Career Development Award • Clinical research training fellowships • Methodology research fellowship
Wellcome Trust www.wellcome.ac.uk	• Career Re-entry Scholarships • Research career development fellowships in basic biomedical science • Wellcome Trust/MIT postdoctoral fellowships • Research Fellowship • Sir Henry Wellcome postdoctoral fellowships

(Continued overleaf)

Table 6.1 Continued

Funding Body	Name or type of scheme
Royal Society www.royalsociety.org	• Dorothy Hodgkin Fellowships • Education Research Fellowships • JSPS Postdoctoral Fellowship Program • University Research Fellowships • Newton International Fellowships
The Leverhulme Trust www.leverhulme.ac.uk	• Early Career Fellowships • Research Fellowships
Royal Commission for the Exhibition of 1851 www.royalcommission1851. org.uk	• Research Fellowships

European Union (EU)
http://erc.europa.eu
http://cordis.europa.eu/fp7/
mariecurieactions
	• ERC Starting Independent Researcher Grant
	• Marie Curie Career Integration Grants
	• Marie Curie International Outgoing
	  Fellowships
	• Marie Curie Intra-European Fellowships
	• Marie Curie International Incoming
	  Fellowships

additional expectation that they are to be employed on the grant for the duration of the award, if it is successful.

The strategy of whether to apply for funding as part of a research team or as an independent researcher also needs careful consideration in terms of who developed the idea (i.e. is it your own research idea, did the idea develop as part of ongoing research between you and your mentor) or whether it is the right time for you from a career development point of view. As an ECR, being part of a research team as a Co-I or researcher co-investigator means that you have the opportunity to learn the process of writing and submitting the grant application as well as doing the research, without the full responsibility and therefore accountability of the PI. Applying for funding as the PI however, even for small grants, allows you to take the lead in shaping the research questions and directions in your field, as well as enhancing your employability prospects. As mentioned earlier, a key part of any research career is the process of applying for funding, and therefore being able to demonstrate this ability as an ECR can give you a competitive employability advantage. [6,7]

As an ECR, one of the more likely research grant applications that you can lead as the PI is the Research Fellowship. Research fellowships focus on the individual's career aspirations as well as the research idea, which makes them a special type of research proposal. A fellowship is more than an opportunity to further existing work of your host laboratory or postdoc project, but rather fellowship schemes for ECRs are usually set up to promote research independence with the expectation that the fellowship and associated resources will help develop and promote you as a future research leader. With a high degree of prestige attached, writing, submitting and securing a fellowship will therefore help boost your career development.

It is worth noting here that applying for funding is an incredibly competitive process, with success rates typically between 15% and 35%.* Unfortunately this means that not all excellent research ideas become successful grant applications. A certain level of 'grantmanship' (Devine 2009) is therefore required to sell your research ideas and expertise to others so that the ultimate decision is to fund your research. In this chapter, it is not our intention to provide a template for a successful application (as this does not exist!); however we aim to describe the common key stages of grant application processes, as well as some top tips. We have tailored this chapter with you playing the role of the lead researcher or PI. Even though this is most likely the case for research fellowships, the key questions identified are relevant to all sorts of grant applications, and so if you are part of a research team, you will see your co-investigators addressing many of the same elements and processes.

Preparation stage

To submit a successful research grant application, such as a fellowship, requires considerable effort in planning and preparation. The time it takes should not be underestimated. It is therefore important to start the preparation early. The whole process leading up to submission can take several months, or longer, as there are many things to consider even before you actually start writing your application.

Key questions that you need to ask yourself include:

- What is your research question or hypothesis?
- What is novel/unique or original about your proposed research?
- Why is it important to do this research – the 'so what' factor?
- What I am going to do to address the research question and what do I need to do it?
- Where will I conduct the research?
- Why am I the best person to carry out this research?
- Who will benefit from conducting this research (and why)?
- Who is likely to fund my research, and am I eligible?

Reif-Lehrer (2000) states that there is no point starting to write a proposal if you cannot come up with positive answers to similar questions to those posed above. The preparation phase is all about 'knowing oneself, the available resources, and

* http://www.epsrc.ac.uk/funding/apprev/successrates/Pages/default.aspx (accessed 2 June 2011)

the "state of the field" ' (Devine 2009). For a grant application where you are part of a research team, the focus of the key questions above becomes more to do with 'we' rather than just 'I', e.g. why are *we* the best team to carry out the research?

What is your research question?

Here you need to think about your research ideas and shaping them into a hypothesis to be tested or a research question to be answered. Chapter 2 provides some detail on choosing your research area, from which your research questions will develop. However, when developing your ideas for your application it is important to keep in mind the length of time of the grant (e.g. 1, 3 or 5 years). This will have some bearing on the magnitude of research question you are trying to address. It is a balance between proposing exciting research that makes a significant contribution versus plans that are too ambitious and not plausible (and therefore not fundable) within the proposed timeframe. For fellowship applications, your research idea also needs to be visionary enough to show how it will develop and mature into your longer term future research career.

This can be quite a step change for a short term/fixed contract researcher and therefore discussing your research ideas with peers and mentors is a good way to gain informal feedback, to develop and hone your ideas further, such as the balance between ambition and feasibility, and to develop your research networks further.

What is novel / unique or original about your proposed research?

To answer this question requires an in-depth knowledge of current literature in your research area. It is therefore perhaps a part of the application process where most ECRs will feel most comfortable. Your PhD has provided you with the necessary skills and training to conduct a comprehensive literature review. For grant applications, you are building on these skills to identify what is new, novel, unique or original about your idea in relation to what has already been done. This exercise is also useful in identifying any potential collaborators or competitors.

Why is it important to do this research – the 'so what' factor?

A research grant application is an opportunity for you to sell your ideas and expertise to others. Not all applications need to 'cure cancer' or 'stop global warming' but you need to put your research into the wider context. You not only need to show that you have a good idea, but that it is something worth doing, and therefore something worth funding. It is also important to show that it is something worth doing now – i.e. that your work is timely. This could be related to pressing global challenges, enhancing an internationally competitive research edge or the recent invention of a new instrument.

What I am going to do to address the research question and what do I need to do it?

This question is all about articulating your research plan and therefore needs to consider the following aspects:

- What are your specific objectives to address your research question?
- What research method will you use and why?
- How long will it take?
- Do you need specialised facilities to conduct the work? Have you arranged access to these facilities?
- Will you need to buy additional equipment, consumables, etc. to carry out the research; if so what, why and how much do they cost?
- Where will the work be carried out?

Devine (2009) suggests conducting an assessment of the institution in which you want to carry out your research as part of the preparation phase, e.g. do they have the right resources (e.g. access to equipment, specialised laboratory space, journal and book collections) for you to be able to conduct your research. For research fellowship applications it is also worth assessing whether the institution offers any career development support or opportunities for research fellows, e.g. will you be able to supervise students and/or attend staff development courses.

As part of the research plan, you will need to provide detailed budgets and justifications for the resources you are requesting, which may even include a salary for yourself. You therefore need to calculate the cost of your proposed research. You may never have had to cost your research before, as it was the responsibility of your research mentor or PhD supervisor, and therefore it is worth seeking help. Key things to look out for are, what can you ask for, e.g. what costs are eligible (e.g. equipment) or not eligible (e.g. studentships) for the particular scheme, what costs are directly allocated (e.g. investigator time) versus directly incurred (e.g. postdoc salary), are there any institutional overhead costs, do you need to provide matched funding? Often universities have online tools to help calculate the costs. Usually you will need to gain institutional authorisation for your estimate before you apply for the funding. As well as your research mentor, your department may have an accounts manager that will be able to help, as well as central administration services within your institution.

Why am I the best person to carry out this research?

As part of the preparation phase, Devine (2009) also suggests a period of self-assessment to identify your own research interests (see Chapter 2) as well as your professional strengths, expertise and past experiences. This period of self-assessment helps you to identify whether you have the necessary skills and expertise to carry out your proposed project. It is your opportunity to identify your unique selling point, and professional strengths over potential competitors. For collaborative projects, it is an opportunity to identify the strengths of the team as a whole.

Who will benefit from conducting this research (and why)?

Beneficiaries of research can be academic, social, environmental, and/or economical, depending on the research area and expected outcomes. As research fellowships are about developing research independence and supporting future research leaders, a potential beneficiary for fellowship applications is also you. Dissemination plans are an important component of your application. If you were a business, seeking investors to fund your new idea, the investors would want to see a return on their investment (Devine 2009). Identifying who the potential beneficiaries are and how they will benefit from your research in the short, medium or long term is a way of demonstrating the potential impact of your research in the wider community.

Who is likely to fund my idea and am I eligible?

There are many funding opportunities to support research (see Table 6.1 for some examples) and it is therefore important to spend the time exploring the research funding priorities of the different schemes. These are usually prominently displayed on the websites of the different funding bodies. This will help you determine whether your research idea fits within their remit and therefore whether they would be willing to fund your research. It is also possible to get an idea of the type of research that is supported by a particular funding body by looking at previous successful applications. UK research councils have online tools available to search for previously awarded grants (e.g. http://www.bbsrc.ac.uk/pa/grants/default.aspx for Biotechnological and Biological Sciences Research Council [BBSRC] and http://gow.epsrc.ac.uk/ for Engineering and Physical Sciences Research Council [EPSRC]). There are also similar databases for US funding agencies (e.g. http://www-commons.cit.nih.gov/crisp for projects funded by the National Institute of Health [NIH]) and EU funding (http://cordis.europa.eu/fp7/dc/index.cfm). Contacts within specific funding bodies can also provide advice on whether your research idea fits within their remit.

Not only is the research remit important, but you also need to check the eligibility criteria of each scheme. These can be based around nationality, level of experience, including the number of years since submitting a PhD, where the research will be conducted, as well as what type of resources that can be requested to support the application. If you are unsure as to whether you are eligible for a particular scheme, or what resources can be requested, it is worth contacting the funding body for clarification. If you are not eligible, based on the rules for the particular scheme, then there is no point applying. If however, you have confirmation from the funding body that you are eligible, it is worth including this information, and the name of your contact within the organisation, in a cover letter with your application.

Top tips for preparation

- Start early. Some applications have fixed submission deadlines and you need to give yourself enough time to do everything.
- Be clear about your research idea and how you will address it, why it is worth funding, its timeliness, what are the benefits, and if it is plausible in the timeframe.
- Be clear about your skills and expertise, and your unique selling point for conducting the research.
- Read the eligibility criteria closely and make sure your research is within the scheme's remit.
- Know what type of things you can ask for, e.g. eligible costs such as equipment, studentships, staff time, etc. Sounds simple but don't ask for things that are not eligible.
- Seek advice on how to cost your research and gain institutional authorisation.
- Investigate whether your department, institution, or even particular funding bodies run workshops on writing fellowships or proposals.

Submission and application process

> A succinct writing style, well-formulated hypotheses, evidence of past productivity, and knowledge of proposed analytical techniques, as well as good grammar and correct spelling are essential.
>
> (Devine 2009: 584)

No matter how many pages the research proposal is supposed to be, in general your answers to key questions identified as part of the preparation phase above need to be included, but written in a language and style that is accessible for a well-educated general reader. The balance between the amount of detail given to any particular component will be specified by the particular funding scheme. A common mistake by novice proposal writers is to place too much emphasis on the background, or to fail to give sufficient attention to meeting non-technical criteria such as resources or management. It is useful to look at previous successful grant applications, as well as the particular assessment criteria, when preparing your application. This will give strong indications of the style, type and balance of information that is required. Looking at the assessment criteria, which can be obtained from the funding body, will show you how your proposal will be judged.

The specific format of the application is dependent on the funding body and the particular scheme. There are usually very specific instructions of what should or should not be included in your application, and in what format. There are also usually specific instructions on minimum font size, margin width, page length and submission deadline. Similar to submitting papers for publication in journals, you must familiarise yourself with these instructions and follow them explicitly. Submissions that do not follow these instructions, or have not included all the necessary information in the right format, will falter at the first hurdle.

Once you have a working document, it is useful to get feedback before submission. Three types of reviewers identified by Reif-Lehrer (2000) include:

1   Someone who also conducts research in your specialist field. This person can provide advice on the research area, appropriateness of the methodology, context against the 'state-of-the-art'. It could also be useful to give this reviewer a copy of the assessment criteria so that they can judge your proposal against these important elements.
2   Someone who conducts research but not necessarily in your specialist field. This person could be from a related subject area. They are able to provide advice on whether your proposal makes sense as it is presented, are the arguments clear and logical, does it have the 'so what' factor?
3   Someone who is good at editing who can provide advice on ways to make the fellowship easier to read and understand.

Kreeger (2003) also suggests showing early drafts to friends or family to ensure that the basic ideas are accessible to non-researchers, ensuring that the proposal is clear to understand. This is particularly true for elements of your proposal such as the general summary and likely impact of your research.

When you have the final Word document and necessary attachments, you will need to navigate the completion of the necessary forms and be familiar with your university's submission process. For online submission, it may need to go through other levels of checks and signatures (e.g. approval by Head of Department, approval by central university administration services) before it is submitted to the funding body. This will take time, and a proposal is not officially submitted until all the necessary levels of approval have been received. If the submission process is online, make sure that you have the necessary access rights and passwords set up in good time.

Before submission, check (Kreeger 2003):

• Have you filled out the forms correctly?
• Have you checked your form for spelling and grammatical mistakes?
• Have you followed the instructions of the funding body explicitly, paying attention to every detail?

Top tips for submission and application stage

• Again start early. Just having a finished Word document is not the end. There are forms to fill in, budgets to upload, letters of support to gather, signatures to chase, etc. This can take several days to weeks to complete. Don't under-estimate how long it will take.

- Follow the instructions or guidelines on what is required to be included in your proposal submission explicitly. Note the date and time for submission. Proposals have been rejected if guidelines are not followed properly. Proposals are not considered after the due date.
- Read copies of successful proposals to gauge the style and layout.
- Know how your proposal will be judged, i.e. get a copy of the assessment criteria, as this will help you to know what criteria are important for this funding body and/or funding scheme.
- Know the process of submitting proposals, identify who else needs to approve it, and warn them in advance.
- For online submission processes, make sure you have the necessary access rights.

Review, response and decision-making stage

Once the proposal has been submitted, it is cause for a celebration. It has been a lengthy process with months of hard work to pull all the necessary information together and submit on time. Once submitted, your application will go through a series of steps, managed by the funding body, before you know the outcome. In general the keys steps are shown in Figure 6.1.

Depending on the specific funding body and the type of application, this process can take several months, or even longer. Whilst we have presented the review process as 5 key steps, different schemes may have fewer, additional or different steps. The make-up of the panel may also differ between different funding bodies. It is therefore important to investigate how the decision will be made about your grant application from the specific funding body you are applying to. This type of information is normally presented on their website, or it is possible to contact the funding bodies directly (e.g. http://www.epsrc.ac.uk/funding/apprev/Pages/default.aspx).

In the selection process, there are three key elements that require a further note. First, if you are given the opportunity to write a response to the reviewer's comments then you need to respond in a professional manner. Similar to responding to a reviewer's comments about a journal publication (see Chapter 5), whilst you may agree or disagree with the reviewer, it is important that you do not take their comments too personally and that you are not too aggressive in your response. You can also use the response as an opportunity to argue your point again, maybe add more evidence if you have more experiments or made more contacts as well as responding to any specific factual inaccuracies. You need to answer all points of concern, do not just ignore them and hope that they go away.

Second, if you are asked to attend an interview as part of the selection process, this is another opportunity to sell yourself and your idea. If you are given the name of the people that will be at your interview beforehand, then spend some

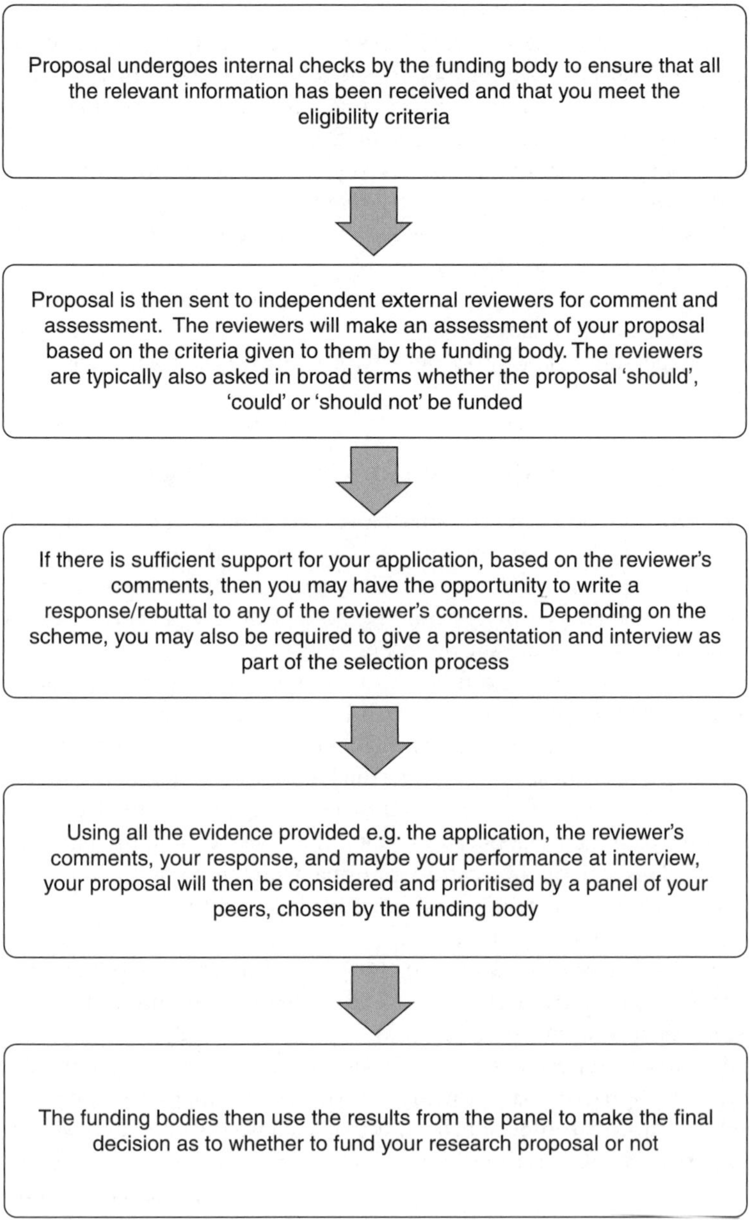

Proposal undergoes internal checks by the funding body to ensure that all the relevant information has been received and that you meet the eligibility criteria

Proposal is then sent to independent external reviewers for comment and assessment. The reviewers will make an assessment of your proposal based on the criteria given to them by the funding body. The reviewers are typically also asked in broad terms whether the proposal 'should', 'could' or 'should not' be funded

If there is sufficient support for your application, based on the reviewer's comments, then you may have the opportunity to write a response/rebuttal to any of the reviewer's concerns. Depending on the scheme, you may also be required to give a presentation and interview as part of the selection process

Using all the evidence provided e.g. the application, the reviewer's comments, your response, and maybe your performance at interview, your proposal will then be considered and prioritised by a panel of your peers, chosen by the funding body

The funding bodies then use the results from the panel to make the final decision as to whether to fund your research proposal or not

Figure 6.1 Key stages of the review and selection process.

time finding out more about their research expertise, as this can give you more idea about the types of questions that they may ask. However, not all members of your interview panel are likely to be experts in your field. So you will need to be able to explain your research in general terms, conveying the importance and impact of the research, without being too overly technical. You should practice your presentation and have a 'mock' interview beforehand. Similar to three types of reviewers identified by Reif-Lehrer (2000) for your grant application, members of your 'mock' interview panel should include:

- Someone who also conducts research in your specialist field. This person will be able to ask you specific questions about your research methodology and approach, probing your level of knowledge of the 'state-of-the-art'.
- Someone who conducts research but not necessarily in your specialist field. This person could be from a related subject area. This person will be able to ask you questions about the importance of the research area and what are the potential benefits and impact.
- Someone who has been through the same or a similar process before. This person will be able to advise you on the process and what to expect.

Third, what happens if your application is rejected? As mentioned at the beginning, not all good research ideas become successful grant applications. If your grant is unsuccessful, it is only natural to get annoyed. You have put a lot of heart and soul into the proposal, spent months preparing it, and months waiting for the decision. However, the reviewer's comments and any further informal or formal feedback from the funding body provide a good source of information as to why it may not have been funded. You can use this feedback to help revise and resubmit your proposal to the same funding body (only if a resubmission is invited) or a different funding body. So it is worth taking another look at the reviewer's comments, e.g. was the approach viewed as technically flawed? If so, fix it with more robust literature or maybe even some preliminary data, or maybe even change the approach. Did the reviewer comment on your lack of expertise? If so, spend time boosting your track record by writing more papers in the area, presenting at conferences, making contacts and networking with people in the field.

When revising a proposal idea with the view of resubmitting, it is also very important to go back to the 'preparation' stage and ask yourself the initial questions again. Perhaps the proposal was not funded because of the way you addressed these questions and therefore you need to think and start again.

Top tips for review, response and decision making stage

- Become familiar with the selection and decision process of the relevant funding body.
- Always be professional in your response/rebuttal to reviewer's comments.

- If necessary, prepare and practice for your interview with a 'mock' interview panel.
- Use the feedback from the reviewers and funding body constructively to help shape future research proposals.

Scenario 6.1 – An excellent research idea is not the full story

Beatrice had completed a PhD and had been working as a postdoc for 2 years. Her aim was to obtain a full time academic post, and her supervisor supported her ambitions and suggested that she apply for a postdoctoral fellowship. There were a range of fellowships available and through discussions with the funders, her mentor and academic and research support staff at her university, Beatrice ascertained that the most appropriate route for her idea and career stage was an EPSRC postdoctoral fellowship. It took nearly a year for Beatrice to develop her idea, consult with leaders and stakeholders in the field, and to develop a very original idea that would have significant academic impact and possible commercial potential. The proposal received very good peer review comments and Beatrice was selected for an interview. She prepared a presentation that summarised her research proposal and went through a dummy run with friends and peers. At the actual interview, Beatrice was surprised to find that none of the panel was a specialist in her field, and came from a very broad range of engineering and science disciplines. She had carefully prepared answers to questions about her research, but many of the questions asked were about how she would convey the impact of her research to a non-specialist audience, her research ambition, project and risk management, people management and her ability to lead a research team. Unfortunately, despite an academically strong proposal, Beatrice did not receive the funding due to her performance at interview.

As Beatrice discovered, success in research, and especially in fellowship competitions, is not only about excellent quality research. Beatrice did the right thing in discussing her proposal with different funders, and taking advice from academic and support staff. However, she needed to research the latter stages of the fellowship application in more detail, by talking to others who have been through this stage and identifying the types of questions asked. She could also have arranged a mock interview and received feedback from academic staff who were not specialists in her field, and who had experience of conducting funding interviews.

Summary

Applying for funding is a key element of a successful research career. The process however requires significant levels of preparation and commitment. As well as having an excellent research idea, successful 'grantmanship' involves being able to convey the excitement, importance, relevance and need of your research idea to both your peers and the funding body. Not all good or even excellent research ideas will be funded, and unfortunately there is no one template for a successful application. However, there are common elements to any grant application that you can consider, which used in combination with a positive reflection of reviewer's feedback from unsuccessful grants may help to boost your experience of the grant writing process.

Recommended/Further reading

Berry, D. C. (2010) *Gaining funding for research: A guide for academics and institutions.* Maidenhead, UK: Open University Press, McGraw-Hill Education.
The book places the grant writing processes within the context of the individual researcher as well as their institution and externally. It is UK-centric in terms of who may fund your research proposal and the review process but provides practical advice on how to get started, costing your proposal and characteristics of successful proposals which are relevant to many different funding bodies.

Reif-Lehrer, L. (2005) *Grant application writer's handbook* (4th ed.). London: Jones and Bartlett Publishers International.
This book splits the grant writing process into key parts such as getting started, understanding the review process, deciphering different aspects of a grant application, planning and writing the research plan and what to do if it is not funded. Each part has a recap section to reinforce the messages. The examples are USA-centric including who may fund your research, types of awards available and example forms, but again the messages are relevant for many different funding bodies.

Chapter 7

Becoming a supervisor

Supervision has always been a part of an ECR's duties, although for most this was generally not formally acknowledged until recently. So a good starting point is to ask what we mean by supervision and what it is that as an ECR you are being asked or expected to do. Once that has been discussed then we can start to consider how you can receive supervisor training or development.

Across the disciplines, it would still appear that for PhD supervision, you can be a member of the supervisory team but not the primary or lead supervisor. Although the Medical Research Council (MRC) doesn't categorically state that, it leaves the decision as to who can be lead supervisor to the institution. As far as we know, most if not all institutions would not allow you to be lead supervisor. Similarly, although the Wellcome Trust is keen to let you gain experience in supervising, by being part of a supervisory team, lack of experience and/or a short term research contract would go against your appointment as lead supervisor.

There are of course other student projects to be involved with such as those for undergraduates and for postgraduate taught programmes. In this context, supervision for science and engineering students can mean day-to-day line management, especially when the main supervisor is not around. As the complexity of the work increases from undergraduate to postgraduate study, supervision may include discussions of the theoretical background to the work and questioning of why particular methodologies are being used. Nevertheless, the prime responsibility for the work will still lie with the principal supervisor. For an ECR though, an advantage of this experience is the excellent background training and preparation for supervision of PhD students.

For ECRs in subjects other than science and engineering, the same is true as they are usually not allowed to be the principal supervisor for any level of dissertation. They might be able to help out doctoral students in particular areas as determined by the principal supervisor, but otherwise, they are much less likely to have the breadth of supervisory experience as is seen with science and engineering ECRs, as there would not be the requirement for help with undergraduate and postgraduate taught dissertations.

The importance of supervision to ECRs has been stressed in a recent Australian study where their two most common additional duties undertaken were informal (day-to-day training and advice) supervision and formal (member of a supervisory panel) supervision (Akerlind 2009: 93).

Where do you start?

A lot depends on how much previous supervisory experience you have. Those ECRs in their first post and especially those from an arts and humanities background may not have much experience at all. In contrast, there may be ECRs who have 5 or more years experience in science and engineering who have been supervising a number of students. So the response to the question will be a variety of answers depending on your background.

Where one begins to have a supervisory role however, is the first experience where you have some level of responsibility towards a student. If you are from a science and engineering background, then the first experience may be in helping undergraduate students. The problem here is that to our knowledge there is little help or guidance provided by institutions for ECRs who help supervise undergraduate and/or Masters projects, and this is probably true for academics too!

An interesting development has taken place at the University of Sheffield Medical School. Called the Sheffield Undergraduate Research Experience (SURE), it attracts undergraduate students who are considering doing a research degree after they graduate. Graduates are offered a 6–8 week summer research project and can be supervised by an ECR who has sole responsibility for the project including grant application, interviewing and budget management. ECRs also benefit by receiving training in recruitment, teaching and supervision, and research project and budget management.

Of course, if you are also a junior academic, then it is highly likely that you will have to undertake some staff training and development which may result in a Certificate in Learning and Teaching (sometimes abbreviated to CiLT) in Higher Education or equivalent. This will usually include some aspects of student supervision.

The student–supervisor relationship

We know that this relationship in particular has always been fundamental to research degree study (Eley and Jennings 2005; Wellington 2010). Specific problem areas in the relationship include: a lack of attention to process issues such as the facilitation of students' acquisition of skills; a confusion over roles especially each others' perceptions of what they should be doing; interpersonal problems possibly relating to cultural differences of overseas students; and the narrowness of the traditional one-to-one supervision relationship.

In addition to some of the above problem areas that might affect the nature of a student–supervisor relationship, there are some potential differences between a more junior ECR and an academic member of staff, which may also have a bearing on the relationship. Such differences include age and experience where academics would more likely be an authority figure. Students may also find that an ECR has more in common with them and because they are less of an authority figure and are perceived as having a lower academic status, they are more approachable. It is likely that you will have more informal meetings with students than academics and see them on a more regular basis. In contrast, academics will usually have more formal meetings and these may be signed off as official records of discussions.

Not surprisingly, with the above potential differences between you and academics, these differences are likely to have an impact on the expectations of the student. Academics might be perceived as more knowledgeable about the research area than you but perhaps less likely to develop a close working relationship with students, given the many other demands on their time. You may find yourself as an apparently approachable supervisor, being confided in about work stresses or personal circumstances, and you will need to be prepared for this mentoring role, and to set clear boundaries that define your professional relationship with your mentees. However, a possible downside for an ECR being too approachable is that you may sometimes not be taken as seriously as an academic.

In pointing out these above differences between ECRs and academics and how they can affect student expectations, any supervisor training or development that you receive would benefit from taking them into account. It is certainly clear that just repeating an academic supervisor training session for ECRs would not be entirely appropriate as the majority of ECRs would in general be less experienced than academic staff and more basic issues relating to the student–supervisor relationship might need further discussion. Moreover, with the more limited experience of ECRs, you may have a greater problem agreeing expectations of students. In general, texts on the subject (Delamont, Atkinson, and Parry 2004; Phillips and Pugh 2010) suggest the following list of expectations are fairly common among supervisors.

Supervisors expect:

- their students to be independent;
- their students to produce good quality written work;
- to have regular meetings with their research students;
- their research students to be honest when reporting on their progress;
- their research students to follow the advice that they give, when it has been at the request of the student;
- their students to be enthusiastic about their work.

However, a major problem for you is that your supervisory role can be very varied, therefore, your expectations of students may be different depending on the role you have been given. Moreover, you might find it more difficult to have an overview of what the overall project is about and all the tasks that the student has to undertake. [8,9]

How can you improve your supervisory activities?

This will obviously depend on your existing knowledge and experience but we will assume that you are a very junior ECR. Although it is very unlikely that you will be able to act as primary supervisor for a doctorate, you will be encouraged to be a co-supervisor or part of the supervisory team. This is useful not only in exposure to the supervisory process but also allows you to benefit from the skills and experience of a senior academic colleague who would act as your mentor. In most institutions you will probably find that in order to be considered as a primary supervisor in the role of a junior academic, experience must have been gained as a co-supervisor for at least one or more students. Being part of a supervisory team will also likely lead to contact with the Departmental Graduate Tutor or equivalent, a person who has a special interest and knowledge of supervisory matters within the institution. In many cases, a Head of Department may also be knowledgeable in this area and offer good advice.

Also at the institutional level, there may be Staff Development Units who run training or development courses on supervision. These are usually for academics but if you have supervisory responsibilities or wish to develop them, you may well be entitled to attend. Moreover, Staff Development Units will often offer tailor-made sessions for departments, so if the Head of Department wanted to include ECRs, then you should also be catered for. Also the CiLT or equivalent has a component on supervision although this course would not be available or relevant to all ECRs. Newer developments to give you the chance to act as Principal Investigator (PI) from monies made available from national and institutional schemes also allow first-hand experience of supervision. With the increasing range of workshops now made available to you as part of the institutional development plans, these may also include aspects on supervision.

Many institutions now have a Graduate School or equivalent and they are usually responsible for booklets such as the local 'Code of Practice for Research Degree Programmes'. These should be based on national guidelines such as the Quality Assurance Agency's 'Code of Practice for the Assurance of Academic Quality and Standards in Higher Education. Section 1: Postgraduate Research Programmes' (QAA, 2004), but with a locally relevant flavour. Such booklets are particularly useful for keeping up-to-date with new developments and requirements and give detailed accounts of rules and regulations. Other publications from the Quality Assurance Agency that can be downloaded from their website are also worth consulting. Another more recent development at the institutional level has been the creation of the local Postdoctoral Society. These also offer workshops which are specifically geared to you and should therefore be particularly relevant.

A number of books have been written about student supervision which usually focus on the doctorate but which should be of general interest and include:

- *How to be an effective supervisor: Best practice in research student supervision* (Eley and Murray 2009) – this is largely based on the Precepts of the above 2004 QAA Code of Practice.
- *A handbook for doctoral supervisors* (Taylor and Beasley 2005) – this focuses on the practical needs of supervisors.
- *Effective postgraduate supervision: Improving the student/supervisor relationship* (Eley and Jennings 2005) – this practical guide presents the most frequently encountered difficulties in the student/supervisor relationship.
- *How to get a PhD: A handbook for students and their supervisors* (Philips and Pugh 2010) – a worldwide bestseller that helps supervisors understand their role in the supervisory process.
- *The good supervisor: Supervising postgraduate and undergraduate research for doctoral theses and dissertations* (Wisker 2005) – this book builds on international experiences of good practice in research supervision.
- *Making supervision work for you* (Wellington 2010) – this book explores the 'delicate balance' that is often involved in supervising students.

Of course, there are many more books that are written primarily for students and these are also worthwhile for consultation, especially those by Rowena Murray on *How to write a thesis* (2006), and *How to Survive your Viva* (2009).

A good online source of material is produced by Vitae (www.vitae.ac.uk) and they also organise workshops and conferences which could be useful. Similarly, the UK Council for Graduate Education (UKCGE) (www.ukcge.ac.uk) also publish booklets which may be relevant, as well as organise a series of workshops every year plus conferences.

You can also prepare for your supervisory role by reflecting on your own experience as a doctoral student: what did you learn from your supervisor about structuring tutorials, giving feedback, setting goals and managing a project? If you had a positive working relationship with your supervisor, you will benefit from analysing which aspects of his or her own behaviour were helpful to you, and seeking to replicate this with your own students; if not, you will know what to avoid! Your personal style of interaction may be different from your supervisor's, and there is no suggestion that you should emulate them unquestioningly, but your recent experience of receiving supervision can be a good starting point for defining your new role. In *The unwritten rules of PhD research* (Rugg and Petre 2010), the hidden messages of supervisory behaviour are analysed in ways that might prompt your own self-reflection – as a continuing researcher as well as a new supervisor.

Top tips for supervision

- Even early on in your career, try to gain as much experience as possible by supervising undergraduate and/or postgraduate students and by being part of a supervisory team.

- Volunteer to undertake local and national supervisor training courses.
- Be prepared to read around the subject and familiarise yourself with institutional and/or national guidelines.
- At the start of the supervision process, establish clear student and personal expectations.
- Be aware that the supervisor–student relationship is fundamental to success.
- Know who to consult in the department, such as the Graduate Tutor, if you need to seek advice.
- Have an understanding of project management.
- Have a thorough understanding of ethics, governance and research integrity.

Project management

A fundamental aspect of supervision lies in the management of the research project and it is important to understand key aspects of project management as described below, to allow you to develop into a better supervisor. In addition to the importance of the student–supervisor relationship in the supervisory process, it is just as important to learn the major tools and techniques to plan and manage projects. To help establish a vision for project management, the late Alan Rousseau created the following model (Figure 7.1). The model is a cycle and most people agree that it makes sense to move in a clockwise direction from the most obvious starting point which is Vision – in other words, seeing the end before you begin. The Focus stage is about defining what the end product will be. With a guiding Vision and specific Focus we now have direction. Once the end product has been agreed, a Plan can be put together, and having broken the work down into bite-size pieces, we can then determine the order, the sequence in which the work is to be done and represent this on a flow chart. Finally, we can create a schedule, a timeline such as a Gantt Chart (Figure 7.2) and this schedule provides the structure on which to base day-to-day management.

The project management model then shows that momentum and motivation underpin the Action stage. Keep Score is about monitoring progress against for example, time or budget. It's also about responding to obstacles and setbacks and about controlling the process by which we make changes to the Plan. At this stage we can see whether we delivered what we promised at the agreed goals of the Focus. This helps us review and Learn from our experience which contributes to our ever-evolving Vision. We can then move round the cycle again and agree new goals for the next phase.

Another model for project management, which is designed to analyse and represent the tasks involved in completing a given project, is known as the Programme (or Project) Evaluation and Review Technique (PERT). It is commonly used with the Critical Path Method (CPM), facilitates decision making and can display more information than the Gantt Chart. Moreover, where a Gantt Chart usually consists of a graph of horizontal bars that depict the start

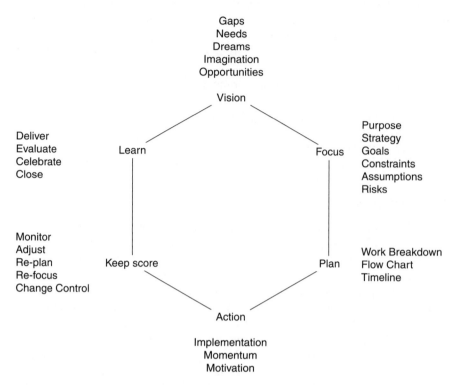

Figure 7.1 A Model for Project Management. From the estate of the late Alan Rousseau.

date and duration for each activity, a PERT Chart usually contains circles and/or rectangles (Figure 7.3).

Apart from the physical mapping of activities related to project management, the nature of some of the activities requires some knowledge for appropriate implementation. Examples include recruitment, where an understanding of

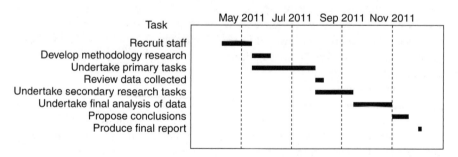

Figure 7.2 Gantt Chart.

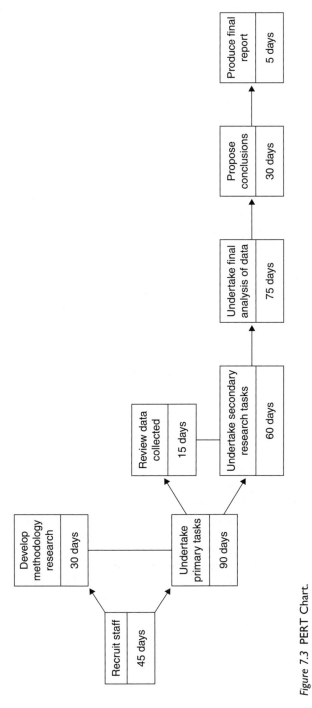

Figure 7.3 PERT Chart.

institutional procedures are required as well as the relevant contacts in the Department of Human Resources (or equivalent), and a reasonable working knowledge and understanding of budgets.

Ethics, governance and research integrity

When it comes to the actual details of the research project, increasingly, a consideration of the ethical issues and research governance has taken on a much higher profile in the last few years and not only in medicine and science. At the same time, an emphasis on matters relating to research integrity has also been highlighted. In the context of supervision, you need to have a thorough understanding of all these matters as well as being of relevance to your own research.

There has been a longstanding ethical responsibility for medical researchers to protect participants from any harm arising from research. However, in the UK following legislation, including the Medicines for Human Use (Clinical Trials) Regulations 2004 and the Human Tissue Act 2004, universities are now required to have ethical approval procedures and a research governance framework in place. The significant changes have been that ethical approval procedures are not solely the responsibility of hospitals and that researchers in the arts and humanities and social sciences now require ethical approval for many of their research activities including completion of questionnaires by participants. As well as harm to participants, ethical approval is also required if the research creates a potential risk to the safety of the researcher or research team. Moreover, in all these matters the responsibility for seeking ethical approval is with the person proposing the research.

The Economic and Social Research Council (2010) have devised a framework for research ethics that serves as a useful example for discussing a range of ethical issues including their six key principles of ethical research which are as follows:

1   Research should be designed, reviewed and undertaken to ensure integrity, quality and transparency.
2   Research staff and participants must normally be informed fully about the purpose, methods and intended possible uses of the research, what their participation in the research entails and what risks, if any, are involved.
3   The confidentiality of information supplied by research participants and the anonymity of respondents should be respected.
4   Research participants must take part voluntarily, free from any coercion.
5   Harm to research participants must be avoided in all instances.
6   The independence of research must be clear, and any conflicts of interest or partiality must be explicit.

To give an idea of whether ethical approval is required for a research project and if so what it entails, a flow chart is given of the ethics review process (Figure 7.4).

Is this research (see glossary)?

Yes   No ⟶   Professional codes of practice still apply
↓

Does proposal address subject of ethics?

Yes   No ⟶   Principal Investigator to write Ethics Discussion
↓

Does it involve more than minimal risk (see Section 1 of Framework for Research Ethics)?

Yes   No ⟶   Review by 'Light touch' Department REC
↓

Does the research involves NHS patients, records, equipment, premises or vulnerable people under the Mental Capacity Act 2005?

No   Yes ⟶   Review by NHS NRES
↓

Are there approved protocols for handling this research situation that are appropriate to current research?

No   Yes ⟶   Light touch review
↓

Send application to appropriate REC for full review
↓

Are there possible conflicts of interest or an appeal?   ⟶   Review by University REC

Figure 7.4 Flowchart of ethics review process. Modified from Engineering and Physical Sciences Research Council (2010) *Framework for Research Ethics*, p. 38 (http://www.esrcsocietytoday.ac.uk/_images/Framework_for_Research_Ethics_tcm8-4586.pdf).

Notes
'Research' is defined as any form of disciplined inquiry that aims to contribute to a body of knowledge or theory.
REC = Research Ethics Committee.
NREC = National Research Ethics Committee.

The ESRC in 2005 made a helpful distinction between ethics and research governance in the following statement.

While ethical principles and review concern the rights, dignity and safety of research subjects, research governance concerns the development of shared standards and mechanisms that permit the proper management and monitoring of research and, if necessary, allow sanctions to be brought in cases of research misconduct

(Economic and Social Research Council 2005: 23)

The ESRC presumes that a research organisation has:

- mechanisms in place to enable timely and expedited review of research and research proposals;
- procedures that are flexible and sensitive to the differing needs of researchers and levels of risk involved in their research;
- procedures to protect the interests of research staff and research students;
- the capacity to deal with cases of research misconduct, complaints and appeals;
- the capacity to advise on statutory or legal considerations that might affect research.

In order to try and prevent cases of research misconduct and to enhance research integrity, in the USA, the National Postdoctoral Association (NPA) has produced a *Responsible conduct of research toolkit* (Flint 2010). The need for such training of postdocs was highlighted in a 2005 nationwide survey (Sigma Xi Postdoc Survey) where 31% of respondents stated that they had received no training in research ethics. The NPA highlights the need for training of postdocs in data acquisition, management, sharing and ownership; mentor/trainee responsibilities; publication practices and responsible authorship, peer review; collaborative science; research misconduct; and communication and difficult conversations. Similarly, in the UK, Research Councils UK (2009) published their code of conduct on the governance of good research conduct.

Work-related stress, bullying and harassment

Although you would probably be aware of these issues in relation to your line manager, once you become a supervisor you have a responsibility towards your students. Under UK law (Health and Safety at Work Act 1974 and Health at Safety at Work Regulations 1999), employers have a legal duty to make sure that employees are not harmed by work-related stress. Although most students would not technically be classed as employees, they have the same rights. Potentially for you, this could be a disciplinary matter.

Likewise, employers are responsible for preventing bullying and harassment in the workplace and it is worth considering the following definitions (Acas 2010) to ensure that you understand what constitutes unreasonable behaviour in this regard.

Bullying is defined as:

Offensive, intimidating, malicious or insulting behaviour, an abuse or misuse of power through means intended to undermine, humiliate, denigrate or injure the recipient.

Harrassment is defined as:

> Unwanted conduct related to a relevant protected characteristic, which has the purpose or effect of violating an individual's dignity or creating an intimidating, hostile, degrading, humiliating or offensive environment for that individual.

Institutions now often run workshops on these subjects and can offer individual guidance and advice and because of your supervisory and other responsibilities, you should be included in mailings to promote such activities.

Interestingly, it was recently reported in the USA that bullying in the workplace is worse among hierarchical industries such as academia, making it a serious cause for concern (*USA Today* 28 December 2010: 28).

Scenario 7.1 – Who is the supervisor?

Dr. Adams had again offered a research project for a potential Masters student as she was always keen to try out new ideas on this type of short-term project. As there were generally few projects relative to the numbers of students needing one, it was almost guaranteed that she would recruit a student. A problem with Dr. Adams was that she tended to over commit herself and she had already agreed to teach a new module overseas at a colleague's institution while the Masters student was going to be in her laboratory. Still, no problem, she knew that she could always rely on her postdoc who was a very obliging Dr. Stevens and as he was seriously thinking about pursuing an academic career himself, he thought that this sort of supervisory experience would stand him in good stead in the future. So almost as soon as the student Ibrahim started, Dr. Adams explained to him that Dr. Stevens was going to play a major role in looking after him, so much so that he was to address all queries to Dr. Stevens as she was going to be away for a while, and then would be extremely busy on her return as she tried to catch up on her other tasks.

As far as Ibrahim was concerned, Dr. Stevens was his *de facto* supervisor although on paper Dr. Adams was the official supervisor, as it was an institutional requirement that the supervisor had to be a member of the academic staff. This seemed a little unfair on Dr. Stevens as he took care of the research planning, helped out in the laboratory and seemed to be responsible for all other matters in the absence of Dr. Adams. Perhaps rather surprisingly, Dr. Adams had even asked if he would like to have experience of managing the thesis write-up, which of course he thought he should agree to, as he was very keen to obtain a good reference from Dr. Adams, should an academic vacancy turn up. Of course, Dr. Adams would have the final look at the thesis as she was obliged to sign it off to show that she was happy with the standard of the student's work. However, all this seemed a bit hard on Dr. Stevens who got no recognition for all this supervisory work and in some ways supervision got in the way of his research and grant writing. But what was he to do? He daren't alienate Dr. Adams and in any case as it had become a departmental expectation of postdocs, he certainly wasn't going to be the one to make a fuss about it. Nevertheless, although ECRs are expected to perform duties in addition to their research, equally they should not end up doing the job of an academic. Although this potentially could be a difficult situation for Dr. Stevens, one possible course of action would be to discuss the matter with the Head of Department to determine whether the initial request from Dr. Adams was reasonable or not.

Scenario 7.2 – There can be more than one relationship

Ahmed had been accepted to undertake a PhD with Prof. Jones, an international authority on waste water treatment and Ahmed was very much looking forward to working with the great man. When Ahmed first met Prof. Jones, he was very impressed with how friendly he was towards him and his family. Ahmed even said to his wife that he couldn't believe how lucky he was to have found such a perfect supervisor. However, after a few weeks, more and more responsibility of dealing with Ahmed was placed on Dr. Waters who was one of Prof. Jones's postdocs. Dr. Waters didn't have a problem with this arrangement as it was an expectation that she should help supervise students. However, Ahmed wasn't entirely happy with the idea as his government was paying large sums of money for his research, which was supposed to be with Prof. Jones. Although Ahmed initially accepted working with Dr. Waters, she wasn't particularly well known in the field and he was beginning to become a little irritated by being told what to do by a woman. So after much consideration, Ahmed went to see Prof. Jones at one of their rare meetings and complained that Dr. Waters was not an appropriate supervisor for him and that unless she was replaced, he would leave the university and take his funds elsewhere.

Prof. Jones was really quite annoyed on hearing the complaint and the timing was terrible as he was just about to go off on a university delegation to Ahmed's country to promote collaboration and to try and secure major research funding. Prof. Jones quickly asked Dr. Waters to come and see him and complained at the mess she had landed him with. Of course, Dr. Waters was shocked and very disappointed too as she had no idea why Ahmed should have made any complaint against her as she thought they had a good working relationship. To try and resolve such a situation, a possible way forward would be to ask all parties to come together and talk frankly (if possible) about their differing expectations and relationships (which ideally should have been done at the outset of the research project) and to see if there was any way forward without the need for Ahmed to leave the institution.

Summary

Perhaps rather naively, becoming a supervisor is thought of as training students how to do research but this is only part of the story. Supervision is as much about teaching and confidence building as it is about research. Moreover, a realisation that the supervisory process can include day-to-day management highlights the importance of project management and related tools such as Gantt and PERT Charts. Finally, for all research projects you need to consider a multitude of responsibilities including ethical implications, governance, research integrity, work-related stress, bullying and harassment.

Recommended/Further reading

Eley, A. and Murray, R. (2009) *How to be an effective supervisor: Best practice in research student supervision.* Maidenhead, UK: Open University Press.
This book is based on the precepts of the Quality Assurance Agency's recent Code of Practice for the Management of Postgraduate Research Programmes. It presents practical information on the QAA Code of Practice, to serve both as a ready reference source for supervisors and as a manual for research supervisor training.

Chapter 8

Becoming a teacher in higher education

Jon Scaife

I told them [my students] that I hadn't the slightest interest in whatever opinions they might have and didn't want to hear any. I told them that while they may have been taught that the purpose of writing is to express oneself, the selves they had were not worth expressing, and that it would be good if they actually learnt something.

(Fish 2008: 5)[1]

Teachers must draw out and work with the pre-existing understandings that their students bring with them.

(Bransford, Brown, and Cocking 2000: 19)[2]

This chapter addresses these questions: Are former ways of university teaching still suitable for today? Are there any alternative ways of teaching that deserve our consideration? Is there any theory about these matters? And are these questions 'merely academic' or can they lead to differences in practice? I hope that the chapter will challenge some of your assumptions about teaching and learning and, by the end, that you will have some different ideas with which to experiment and enrich your university teaching.

Introduction

Think of a class you expect to be teaching in the not too distant future. Perhaps you might consider the topic you'll be teaching or the people in the class. Here's a little challenge: *how will you decide how to teach this class?* Do any of the following responses fit for you: I'll teach it . . .

- by checking I know the material and then delivering it?
- in the way I was taught this topic when I was a student?
- in the way I've taught the topic to the same level of students before?
- in ways I think my colleagues teach topics and cohorts like this?

When you were considering this perhaps some additional ideas emerged. Are there any other factors that you might take into account when thinking about teaching this class?

I will argue in this chapter that a radically different way of thinking about teaching is worth exploring but I do acknowledge that the four approaches above have their appeal. In particular, in each case the teacher has control – total or partial – of the content to be taught. That means the teacher is in a position to make sure in advance that her or his knowledge of the topic is secure. Apart from 'covering' the stipulated curriculum this guards against risks like drying up, losing one's thread or running out of material before the end of the session. It also makes preparation economical in terms of the teacher's time.

Another advantage is that these approaches have been tried before and all have worked, at least adequately, in that students have responded to them as acceptable ways of being taught. Moreover, it is irrefutable that students have learned from classes that have been taught in these ways.

For most of the twentieth century these approaches were adequate; students learned from them, they were probably not seen as priorities for departmental deliberation and they were rarely subjected to formal critical consideration. Today, though, I think these approaches are no longer adequate, for two compelling reasons. The first concerns the population of learners.

I. Changes in the HE student community

Education in the UK is compulsory to age 16 but the *de facto* leaving age for most school students is 17, 18 or 19, as more and more stay on to seek further qualifications. It's hard to make one's way in a contemporary knowledge economy without some extra credentials and with unappealing youth employment prospects, 'staying on' has become not only more attractive but also more necessary. On leaving school and college more students than ever before hope to enter higher education. The total number of students in UK HE in 2009/10 was just under two and a half million (Higher Education Statistics Agency 2011). That represents an increase of a million during the previous 15 years. It is five times the UK student population of the 1960s, an expansion that has come to be known as the 'massification' of Higher Education.

Higher education has become an instrument in people's pursuit of economic viability and the anticipated personal and social benefits that that is taken to confer. Motivation to participate in HE has shifted from the 'intrinsic' towards the 'extrinsic'. Someone is intrinsically motivated to pursue a particular activity if the goal for doing so lies within the field of the activity itself; for example, I practise the violin because when I play better I like the sound more. Engagement in the activity is motivating in itself. This is a 'virtuous circle', a positive feedback loop, with the potential to result in deep learning. On the other hand when the goal lies outside the field of the activity the motivation is extrinsic: I practise the violin because I get presents when I pass violin exams;

I'm more interested in getting the presents than in playing the violin. The result of a shift towards extrinsic motivation is that the 'ends' acquire much more significance than the 'means'. Do any of these questions look familiar: 'Is this on the syllabus? Do we need this for the exam?' How about this lament: 'All they're interested in is what they have to do to pass. They're not motivated.'

Why does the intrinsic–extrinsic difference matter? In an era when the student body was a highly qualified minority, in the sense of having succeeded at school examinations that were constructed largely by HE admissions tutors, on courses that were apprenticeships for HE study, it is unsurprising that teaching approaches like the four listed at the start of the chapter could be employed unproblematically. A-level students were, in effect, groomed for HE study. Students tended to apply for subjects that were of interest to them and towards which they were intrinsically motivated. Almost any teaching approach would have had some success, since much of the energy that drove student learning came from the students themselves. The student population in today's HE institutions has changed. It is more diverse, differently schooled and differently motivated. With these changes the viability of the four 'traditional' teaching approaches has diminished.

It is no longer wise to assume that the majority of students are intrinsically motivated towards study in the subjects they are taking. It makes sense, therefore, to enquire whether there are teaching approaches that incorporate strategies for *generating* intrinsic motivation in students. There may be two immediate objections: (i) it can't be done; and in any case (ii) it's not the teacher's responsibility. Actually we know that it can be done: it *is* possible to enhance students' intrinsic motivation. Good sports teachers and coaches have been doing so for years. For some teachers this has come about through the development of personal, intuitive pedagogic strategies but as I will argue in the following sections, lessons can be learned from these cases and linked to a 'constructivist' perspective on knowing and learning to suggest more widely applicable teaching approaches that aim to build on the knowledge and motivation that learners bring with them.

There are several dimensions to the second objection. One is moral: students apply for our courses in good faith that we will help them to learn; we offer them places knowing this. In making these offers we are entering into a contract with them, our part of which involves helping them to succeed by taking reasonable care over our teaching. To put it bluntly, if we don't want to bother with how we teach then surely we shouldn't accept students onto our courses! There's also an instrumental dimension, in which a counter argument might be this: academic staff have a major responsibility for the academic standing and reputation of the department. The department's standing or, if you prefer, its market position, will suffer if student experiences of teaching are poor. Therefore HE teachers have a major responsibility for looking after the quality of their teaching.

2. Changes in views about knowledge and learning

Consider the following summary of an approach sometimes known as 'transmission teaching': 'I am highly knowledgeable about discipline X. I will tell you lots of true things about X. Your job is to learn these things.' I suspect that was the tacit position taken by my undergraduate lecturers in the 1970s. A problem with this is that students are expected to learn uncritically, for reasons of social leverage. Learning is supposed to occur simply because the lecturer occupies the epistemic high ground. Learners are complicit in this arrangement. By accepting a passive role they avoid taking responsibility for critical consideration of what and how they are being asked to learn. They expect tutors to specify both course content and teaching approach, a position that gives tutors the comfort of being in control.

In the absence of intrinsic motivation to learn, transmission teaching all too readily results in 'cosmetic', or 'surface learning' (Biggs and Tang 2007; Marton and Saljo 1976). In the field of science education, for instance, there are abundant published examples of learners who can recite apparently sound scientific accounts but who, on being quizzed a little further, reveal deep misconceptions in those same areas of science. They have learnt key words, laws and processes but haven't joined them up into a coherently understood web of knowledge. This even holds for graduates (Bonello and Scaife 2009; Scaife 2007a, 2007b).

A major challenge to a transmission approach to teaching is that, as our culture has become increasingly diverse and pluralistic, we have become less inclined simply to trust the word of experts. It no longer works to tell students, 'learn this because it's true – I say so'. Knowledge is contested and students are more willing than they used to be to hold on to ideas that run counter to those declared by their tutors. To deal with this they have learnt to occupy two epistemic spaces: a personal space in which their ideas fit adequately with their goals and experiences, and a 'student space' in which they know that to succeed when assessed they must report versions of their tutors' ideas.

Constructivism and teaching

There are better ways to teach than through 'transmission'. Today's ECRs are perfectly placed to initiate timely and significant developments in HE teaching.

Suppose someone was coming to visit you and they phoned you for directions, what would you say to them? I imagine that fairly high on your list of priorities would be to ask, 'Where are you?'. In order to guide them it would be natural first try to find out where they were coming from; in other words you would 'diagnose' their position. Teaching that acknowledges and responds to 'where learners are coming from', namely their current knowledge, understanding and feelings of confidence and motivation, is sometimes called diagnostic teaching (DT). In purposefully taking account of where learners are, DT is radically different from transmission teaching. [10]

A pragmatic argument for DT is that by investigating students' learning needs we can target our teaching, giving greatest emphasis to areas of greatest need. A psychological argument for DT derives from a contemporary view of knowing and learning called constructivism. There are several versions of constructivism but all have in common the assertion that learning is a process of knowledge construction, as opposed to a process of receiving pre-formed knowledge. The latter view is consistent with a 'blank slate' model of the mind. Just such a model was proposed, largely for egalitarian reasons, by the English philosopher John Locke a little over 300 years ago. The blank slate model in turn suggested a pedagogy of transmission, in which important ideas were to be transmitted (today we say lectured, professed or disseminated) to students by scholars. It was assumed that students would learn by reception of these ideas, an assumption that could be checked by assessing the extent to which students could replicate them. These days it is easy to be sceptical about a transmission view of teaching; in particular we know only too well that telling things to people by no means guarantees that they will know, remember, believe or perhaps even hear them. Despite this fairly obvious observation, transmission teaching is alive and well in our universities and schools. How can this be? One reason is that it is the devil we know. Most of us were probably taught through transmission and since we managed well enough we probably weren't particularly critical or even aware of the shortcomings of the method. Another reason was raised earlier, in connection with the four teaching approaches introduced at the start: in transmission mode the teacher is largely in control and is thus relatively protected from embarrassing situations such as drying up or revealing lack of knowledge about something. The fact that people don't learn very well by just being told things is often outweighed by these considerations.

Locke didn't offer a pedagogic argument for transmission teaching. He didn't need to. The method was regarded as a natural way of spreading knowledge from experts to the less knowledgeable. Knowledge was disseminated by oratory and through the distribution of 'great books'. In contrast, if we look at the emergence of constructivist ideas 200 years after Locke, persuasive arguments for describing learning from a constructivist perspective were given by two major contributors to twentieth century cognitive psychology, Jean Piaget and Lev Vygotsky. Space in this chapter permits the inclusion of some central constructivist ideas and an exploration of implications of constructivism for teaching but not a substantive account of constructivism itself. For a fascinating and challenging account of a version of constructivism that has been particularly influential in education see Glasersfeld (1995). Steffe and Gale's (1995) compilation contains contributions from Glasersfeld as well as others with different views of constructivism.

If, as constructivism maintains, learning is a process of knowledge construction, how and from what does this occur? Let's start with the observation that someone can neither know nor make someone else's knowledge for them. To learn about the genesis and growth of a person's knowledge we must look at that person. As each of us navigates our way through daily life we have a stream of experiences. These experiences are the 'materials' from which we construct knowledge. We are never empty-headed as we navigate; we have a dynamic stock of knowledge. We use our knowledge in a myriad of ways, one of which is to make sense of some of our experiences. The sense we make is internal to us; what we make of an experience is made in relation to what we already know. Imagine someone seeing a car hurtling down a road. What are they to make of it? Three people with their own distinct stocks of knowledge are a police officer, a cyclist and a formula one motor racing enthusiast. I expect they would make quite different meanings from the sight of a hurtling car. Current knowledge is the set of 'tools' with which we make new knowledge from our experiences. Perhaps this is not so surprising, since if one is willing to treat learning as a process of building or construction then it seems difficult to imagine anything other than current knowledge being the means by which construction is accomplished. (Here and throughout the chapter I am using the word 'knowledge' as short-hand to refer to anything that teachers may wish to help develop in learners: factual knowledge, understanding, skills, behaviours, values and so on.)

The psychological strand of constructivism of Piaget, Vygotsky, Glasersfeld and others contains a second key claim about learning, namely that if a learner's knowledge fits with her or his goals, values and continuing experiences then the knowledge remains stable or, as Glasersfeld puts it, viable. The remarkable thing about that claim is that it contains no reference to the idea of truth. From a constructivist perspective people maintain their knowledge if it fits for them, not according to whether it is true. Researchers in the fields of public and children's understanding in science are well aware of this. People maintain all sorts of ideas that the scientific community of practice rejects – some people even do this in full knowledge of accepted scientific views – because the knowledge that they have constructed fits better for them than does the accepted scientific account. In the absence of a constructivist perspective we might account for this by saying that such people were ignorant, ill educated or just plain contrary. In the light of constructivism we can see that they are simply maintaining a position of 'personal rationality'. An acknowledgement that learners' alternative ideas, misconceptions and errors are usually not experienced as such by the learners themselves is a significant departure from a standard knowledge-based conceptualisation of teaching. If we respect their alternative ideas as knowledge (or, if you prefer, beliefs) that they have spent their lives building up through their experiences, as opposed to dismissing them as simply wrong, then the challenge of trying to teach begins to take on a new shape. We know that learners come to us with prior ideas and that they are liable to hold on to them if we just try to 'overwrite them' with our own knowledge. A constructivist understanding of teaching suggests that a teacher's energies are better directed towards persuasion than to transmitting information; better in the sense of being likely to lead to authentic, as opposed to cosmetic, learning. Constructivism implies a 'pedagogy of persuasion'. The design problem is then this: what moves can teachers make that are conducive to persuading learners to change their minds?

Scenario 8.1 – Why won't you just tell us?

Linda taught undergraduate engineers. To follow up on lectures, students were given problems to tackle and they brought their answers to tutorials. Linda found that students were often successful at problems that required them to lift material more or less directly from their lectures. But when it came to applications of underlying principles they were far less assured. Linda had a particular interest in the historical development of knowledge in her subject. She felt that if students saw where key principles came from they might gain a deeper understanding of their applicability. She decided to teach a topic using a historical account. It didn't go well. Not only did students struggle with the problems as before but they resented what they saw as her teaching 'beyond the course'. She came to realise that though a historical account made good sense to her this was no indication that students would see it that way.

Some time later Linda came across the idea of diagnostic teaching. Since her students continued to struggle with the 'application' problems she decided to explore the ways they were thinking when they addressed these problems. She broke down some of the longer problems into sequences of true/false questions and put them to students in her tutorials. After someone gave a true or false answer she asked the others for their views. They were suspicious and wanted her to tell them the right answer. She resisted and instead asked them to say how they had reached their true or false decisions. They didn't think much of that; why bother with their flaky ideas – why not just tell them the answer? That's what teachers are supposed to do, isn't it? She persisted. The students came to see that she was actually interested in their ideas and would not criticise them for 'getting it wrong'. This encouraged them to be more forthcoming and, not surprisingly, they started reporting ideas that challenged each other's thinking. Peer teaching started happening. Gradually the focus in Linda's tutorials shifted from knowing to thinking.

Inquiry based teaching

> What I am arguing is for seeing both research and teaching as different forms of inquiry.
>
> (Bradley 2002: 451)

If we opt for a pedagogy of persuasion we need to know where to start: what are we up against? Another way of putting this is that it would be useful to diagnose our students' learning needs. This is inquiry-based teaching, in which the challenge for the teacher is to elicit learners' knowledge in the discipline, as opposed to eliciting from them utterances that they believe we teachers want to hear. Learners will have varying degrees of confidence in their own knowledge and when they feel insecure they may be fearful of embarrassing themselves through revealing 'unacceptable' or 'wrong' ideas. Those, though, are the very ideas that will inform us about their learning needs! We need to gain their trust and convince them that their ideas have value for us, to help them overcome apprehensions about looking silly in front of their peers. There are moves that teachers can make towards this end. One is to explain to learners why it is useful for you, the teacher, to learn about their ideas, both right and wrong. If you had no idea what their learning needs were you would have to guess or perhaps resort to one of the four strategies listed in this chapter's introduction. They will probably agree that teaching that is aimed towards their learning needs is a better bet for all concerned.

Another move is to get learners talking about aspects of the subject matter. This has three benefits: (i) by expressing ideas in language, as opposed to fluid unspoken thought, learners are carrying out a creative process of synthesising their 'position statements'; (ii) by exchanging position statements with their peers they are encountering alternative views and experiencing challenges to some of their own ideas, which may be a first step towards changing their ideas; (iii) by listening to them you are able to learn about their current ideas, ask for elaboration and make judgements about their learning needs. Since learners of all ages can be reluctant to air their views in front of a class, whole-class questions are not particularly conducive to diagnosing learning needs. The psychologically safest context in which to speak up is probably with an immediate neighbour; students in my classes become very used to me saying, 'see what your neighbour thinks about this and tell them what you think'.

Another diagnostic questioning strategy is to include a 'third party' in the questions: rather than asking people directly for their particular ideas, which can generate stress if the respondent is not confident about the issue, a teacher can bring in an extra character, perhaps like this: 'Imagine that you have a younger brother or sister who is doing Hamlet at school. If they asked you why you think Hamlet rejected Ophelia what would you say to them?' This 'third party strategy' creates a safer space in which learners can frame their thoughts. It also emphasises that it is *their* views that are being sought, not some hypothetical right answer; the use of 'you' and 'your' reinforces that position.

A fruitful diagnostic strategy is to ask students to tackle some tasks and puzzles on the subject in question. I employ this in order to identify graduate scientists' learning needs in school physics, an area about which many beginning teachers are very apprehensive. I introduce them to the idea of diagnostic assessment and explain my purpose in using it. I emphasise that the set of tasks is a survey, not a test, and to reinforce the point that I am interested in their personal beliefs I invite them to respond anonymously if they wish. In the event, every year almost all of them do add their names, principally so that they can have their surveys returned after I have analysed their responses. I use the analysis to identify the topics and themes in which the group as a whole has performed least well and in which they have declared the lowest confidence in their responses. This defines their learning needs and specifies my priority teaching topics.

When I return their surveys and we look at one of the puzzles in a priority topic area they quickly start comparing their own responses with those of their neighbours. What happens next I find interesting and, from a teaching perspective, particularly pleasing: they start peer teaching. 'Why did you put that?' 'I thought it was this.' 'What did you put for that one? How come?' Participating in the diagnostic task results in them becoming stakeholders in their responses. They become intrinsically motivated and curious to learn, and they set about doing just that, from each other.

I have observed ECRs, who were participating in courses for new HE teachers, harness the power of peer feedback on project work in architecture and in music composition. In each case a casual observer could have been forgiven for wondering at first whether *anybody* was teaching or learning, so different was the social dynamic from normal transmission teaching. Yet the level of engagement was high and in due course impressive products of creative energy and critically reflective thought emerged from a collaborative process in which *everyone* was a teacher and a learner.

When I first started using diagnostic surveys in a systematic way I didn't anticipate the impact of the 'formative' spin-off. Now I see it as a major benefit of the approach. If teachers are concerned that systematic diagnostic assessment (DA) might eat into their teaching time I encourage them to treat diagnostic teaching as an inquiry process and see what happens. I am confident that they will find the payback from DA in the form of peer teaching and learning more than offsets any 'lost' time.

Support for DA can be found in the conclusions drawn from a very large-scale meta-analysis of factors influencing teacher effectiveness carried out by John Hattie (2009). Hattie's analysis involved data generated from several million students in over 50,000 studies. He observed that, 'The most powerful single influence enhancing achievement is feedback . . . the most important feature was the creation of situations in classrooms for the teachers to receive more feedback' (p.12). The feedback to which Hattie is referring is diagnostic feedback.

To summarise, DA enhances achievement because (i) it enables teaching to be targeted towards learning needs; (ii) it shows learners that their ideas count for something – that they matter to the teacher; (iii) it heightens curiosity about the topics being studied; (iv) it opens up rich opportunities for peer teaching and learning.

So far I have argued that a constructivist-informed approach to teaching is likely to be more fruitful in terms of student learning than a traditional transmission approach. A constructivist-based pedagogy of persuasion involves inquiry teaching from the outset, so that the teacher can identify learners' learning needs. What next?

After learning needs have been identified the teacher could start trying to address those needs by providing appropriate information to the students. A constructivist-informed alternative is to maintain the stance of teaching as inquiry. The challenge for the teacher is then this: having identified the students' main learning needs, what experiences can I design for them that will lead them to see value in changing their ideas? The teacher accepts that he or she can't change the learners' ideas for them but can create conditions in which they might be persuaded to do so themselves. The details of any such conditions will vary with students' particular learning needs and with the discipline area. That's why there isn't a prescriptive list of 'top tips for teaching' in this chapter. But are there any general principles that can guide teachers who are trying to persuade learners to change and develop their ideas? Here are some suggestions.

1   Learner engagement is almost certainly a necessary condition for 'deep', as opposed to 'surface learning'. We know that people differ from each other and vary over time in their dominant attentional modalities. The implication for teaching is that variety is worthwhile in itself. Just doing something out of the ordinary may reach some learners who would otherwise be detached from current events in a classroom. This is an alibi for unfettered teacher creativity! I once taught a physics course whose authors must have known this; to introduce the concept of polarisation of waves they invited the teacher to lie down in a horizontal position and enquire whether the students could see her/him. That is just plain silly from the perspective of formal physics but it makes excellent sense pedagogically; it is likely to generate attention and enable the teacher to prompt thinking and discussion about what polarisation means. It also provides a metonym, a 'hook', for re-visiting the conceptual story that emerges: 'Remember when I lay on the floor and asked if you could see me . . . what was that about? Tell your neighbour what you think.'

2   If a person is being invited to modify her/his views, to accommodate an alternative perspective, the alternative should be both relevant and plausible *to the person*. It can be easy to overlook that it is the *learner's* judgement that will determine what he or she makes of the presented alternatives, not the teacher's judgement. An argument may be elegant, parsimonious, logically irrefutable and directly to the point in the mind of a teacher but that will matter not a jot, as far as authentic learning is concerned, if learners do not see it as making sense. Research into the public understanding of science demonstrates this well: naïve scientific views disappear during secondary school, examinations are passed, science is dropped and the naïve views reappear.

3   Curiosity is part of human nature. The philosopher Daniel Dennett (1991) remarks that we are born with 'epistemic hunger' and we never lose that appetite. It may, though, be all too dormant in class. If we can awaken students' curiosities then we will have their attention. They will also be

disposed to learn, so as to satisfy their curiosity. I have found that a very effective way of stimulating curiosity is to issue gentle challenges. These might be in the form of teasers or they may be presented as invitations to predict something. Here's a puzzle that I sometimes use when teaching about tensions associated with learning: someone says, 'I have two children. One is a girl. What is the likelihood that my other child is a girl too?' Learners find it easy to engage with the puzzle and to give it some thought. Typically they may think, 'It seems like 50-50 but it can't be that easy. What's going on?' Their curiosities have been stirred; they have become 'stakeholders' in the unfolding story. As teachers this is surely just what we want.

Inviting predictions can be a powerful tactic in teaching, especially if the issue under consideration can include something observable. This is frequently the case in practical subjects and can sometimes be engineered in other disciplines. Learners are presented with a situation in which some kind of process will take place and they are invited to predict what will happen. To reduce guessing they are asked to explain their prediction, possibly to their near neighbours. They then observe the process unfold and in doing so they experience a degree of fit or misfit between their prediction and their observation. I call this teaching approach PEOR: Predict, Explain, Observe and then . . . it depends on whether what was observed Reinforces the prediction or necessitates a Re-think. There are many topics that can be taught using PEOR instead of telling. Even if a concrete observation is impossible to arrange, reasoned prediction can be employed to generate peer discussion along the lines of, 'I think X would happen because . . .'; 'Yes, but what about Y? Wouldn't that change things?'

4   Puzzles and surprising observations are situations that lead to learning by generating 'cognitive conflict'. Cognitive conflict is experienced when something unexpected happens. We eschew incoherence in our experiences and are not normally comfortable when 'wrong footed'. Several responses are possible; we may disengage from the experience by distancing ourselves from it. We may re-frame our observation in order to see it as an instance of something familiar, something that fits after all. Piaget called that process 'assimilation'. If we don't or can't adopt either of those two responses we will be faced with a mis-fit that persists until we find a new way to make sense of the novelty. This requires a transformation of our current knowledge, a re-organisation that Piaget called 'accommodation'. Accommodation is a more profound process of learning than assimilation. And therein lies an opportunity for teachers: if we can design situations with which our students will remain engaged and in which they will experience cognitive conflict then they are likely to respond by transforming their knowledge so as to reduce the conflict. One possible way for a teacher to do this is to collect a range of student views about the topic being taught. They could be drawn from a survey or just from your imagination. Students working in small groups are

then invited to make judgements about these views, a process that is likely to highlight differences within the groups. The students' realisation that their own views are far from universally held can be challenging, but because the challenge is from peers rather than from 'authorities' the participants are more likely to remain engaged and open to learning. (A higher stake version of this would be to involve students in role play.) I have observed ECRs fruitfully employing these ways of generating cognitive conflict in classes in archaeology, architecture, biblical studies, dentistry, education, English, geography, history, journalism, landscape, law, philosophy, politics, psychology, town and regional planning and in many science and engineering disciplines. It is worth remarking that in order to design situations that produce cognitive conflict the teacher needs knowledge of students' current ideas, obtained from diagnostic assessment.

Scenario 8.2 – Stilted seminars

Tom held undergraduate politics seminars with groups of about 16 students in an old rectangular shaped room. The tables and chairs occupied by the students were arranged in a long U-shape and the obvious place for the tutor was at the top of the U, at the 'focal point' of the group. He became aware that a pattern had developed in which he would open up a topic, often with a question, and after a short, awkward interval someone would reply, always addressing him. Seminars had the form of stilted conversations between himself and various individuals in front of an unanimated audience. He wasn't happy about this. Tom decided to try different arrangements in the room. He quizzed colleagues about how they used space in their seminar rooms. He experimented by seeing if it made any difference to the dynamic when he stood or sat down. Realising that when he stood he may be leering over those nearest to him and not making good eye contact with them he tried moving further away from the U. This was counter-intuitive to him as he had felt that proximity would help to make the discussion more relaxed. To his surprise when he moved away people seemed to become a little more animated. Pushing the boat out further, he decided that after introducing a topic he would move further away from the U and stand at the board, not making eye contact with students, just waiting. The first silence tested his nerve. When someone spoke he made a few jottings on the board from what the student said and then waited again. Someone else spoke, and then another – not to him but to the previous speaker. He continued to jot, précising what was said, without adding his own judgements. He found that this wasn't a fluke. Something similar could be reproduced in his subsequent seminars. He felt he had learned how to improve the dynamic in his seminars.

Initial and continuing development of teaching

Developing and refreshing one's teaching is much easier when not working alone. There may be formal provision for this in your workplace: since the Dearing Report in 1997 most UK HEIs offer teacher education courses for ECRs and sometimes for graduate teaching assistants. There may also be openings for staff to complete a Masters degree in Education. My experience of programmes like these has been very positive. Participants have consistently welcomed opportunities to learn from each other and to form fruitful alliances for supporting the development of their teaching. If any such programmes are available in your HEI they would be well worth investigating. [11,12]

This final section describes a possible way of collaborating with peers or other colleagues, whether informally or as part of a course, with the aim of supporting the development of each person's teaching. There are, of course, well known ways *not* to do this. Dropping in on someone's class and telling them afterwards what they should have done is one to avoid. Supervision of teaching can, though, be a very fruitful way of developing teaching. When supervision is used for this purpose, as opposed to, say, for performance management or assessment, the intended beneficiary is the teacher. In view of this it makes sense to design the supervision process around the teacher's needs and wishes. An early decision concerns the logistical arrangement preferred by the teacher. Possibilities include live supervision in the classroom, use of a recording (usually made by the teacher her/himself) or the teacher reporting back on aspects of their teaching. Each has its advantages, as discussed in Bonello and Scaife (2009: chapter 5). But before launching into one of these it is well worth preparing the ground by engaging in a 'contracting process' (Bonello and Scaife 2009: chapter 4). This typically takes the form of an advance discussion, with the aims of minimising the risk of misunderstandings and deciding what to do should problems arise during supervision. A scenario may illustrate the value of a contracting discussion: suppose you are live supervising a colleague who would like you to focus on the way students work together in small groups. When group work starts, do you remain separate from the students, do you join a group, or do you move from group to group? If you do visit groups and students start asking you questions what will you do – respond, ignore them, or refer them to the teacher? These issues can be clarified through a contracting meeting, without which you might make decisions that conflict with the teacher's wishes.

Another useful move during contracting is to agree one or more focuses for the supervision session and here again it is important to prioritise the teacher's wishes. If the teacher is concerned about, say, the clarity of her or his explanations then supervision will be useful if this is addressed. That is not to say that the supervisor's judgements and priorities are to be ignored – and that is another issue for contracting.

Having agreed to focus on the teacher's preferred themes the colleagues might explore how to manage any other issues that emerge for the supervisor. It is unwise for the supervisor to railroad such issues into the session regardless of the teacher's wishes, since that might undermine the quality of the teacher–supervisor relationship and generate a defensive response. It may help the supervisor to hold on to the idea that her/his main aim is to facilitate a colleague's learning, something that is rarely achieved just by telling.

After an 'observation' stage (whether live, from recording or from reporting) comes a discussion or debrief. In the debrief teachers sometimes ask, 'Well what did you think of that?' While I wouldn't ignore that request I think there is much to say for pre-empting it by starting a debrief by asking the teacher how *they* felt about the session; for instance, what did they feel worked well? What would they do similarly again? What would they change? (and what prompts them to feel a change might be appropriate?). In taking a questioning and listening role the supervisor is encouraging the teacher to reflect, to analyse what went on and to make judgements, rather than relying on the supervisor to do that for them. Further discussion about a range of possible supervisory roles (not role plays; rather ways of behaving in the debrief) can be found in Bonello and Scaife (2009, chapter 5).

A final word on development of teaching through collegial supervision: my experience has been that the supervisor generally learns just as much as the teacher from the process. That was reflected in over 10 years of participant evaluations in a teacher education programme for intending HE teachers (Harland and Scaife 2010): consistently the most highly rated aspect of the course was peer supervision of teaching.

Summary

The student population has changed since the time when many of today's university teachers were students. Knowledge is contested; the views of experts are seen as situated perspectives, not as ultimate insights about reality. Teaching methods that once were adequate may no longer be fit for the purpose of motivating and educating a population that is more diverse than ever before. A constructivist perspective on learning and a corresponding inquiry approach to teaching open up alternative approaches to traditional 'transmission' teaching. Constructivism provides a foundation for many practical applications in teaching. Teachers' own learning needs can be addressed through a constructivist-based, collegial approach to supervision.

Notes

1 Stanley Fish, Dean Emeritus at the College of Liberal Arts and Sciences, University of Illinois.
2 John Bransford, Co-chair, Committee on Developments in the Science of Learning and Committee on Learning Research and Educational Practice.

Recommended/Further reading

Books

Biggs, J. and Tang, C. (2007) *Teaching for quality learning at university.* Maidenhead, UK: Open University Press.
Describes what it says on the cover. Discusses Biggs' useful idea of 'constructive alignment' between assessment, teaching and learning, arguing that unless these things are purposefully aligned in course design, students will direct their energies towards surface learning for marks, as opposed to learning for understanding.

Leamnson, R. (1999) *Thinking about teaching and learning.* Stoke-on-Trent, UK: Trentham Books.
Focusing on teaching first year undergraduates. Leamnson is a scientist though his account is applicable to a wide range of disciplines.

Ramsden, P. (2003) *Learning to teach in higher education* (2nd ed.). London: Routledge/Falmer.
This has become a core text in the field of teaching in HE. Easy to read and to browse. Strong on links between assessment and learning, and between both of these and teaching.

Chapter 9

Developing your career

Having considered the many roles and skills demanded of an ECR, in this chapter we consider how these might shape your future career. A fundamental question for you is how to find out what career opportunities may be available. Also, in the event that you want to pursue an academic career, what must you do to give yourself the best possible chance of achieving it? Lastly, so that you can allow yourself to reach your full career potential, can any specific support needs be met by your institution?

The vast majority of ECRs will have progressed from undertaking an undergraduate degree to postgraduate degree(s) and even to their first postdoctoral position, possibly without really thinking where their career path was taking them. In some cases, it is even possible to undertake all three roles within the same institution. So in many instances, when you become an ECR, this may be the first time that any serious thought has been given to contemplate what might happen next. Moreover, it is important that some sort of career plan be constructed at this stage if not before, as generally one really will need to be proactive to take your career in a certain direction. Thankfully, over the last 10 to 20 years in the UK there have been a number of major initiatives both at national and local levels to help you in your choice of career and in the provision of career advice.

The Research Councils which support over 30,000 researchers at any one time have created a Research Councils UK Research Careers and Diversity Strategy (http://www.rcuk.ac.uk/rescareer/rcdu/default.htm) which has the following three aims:

1 to ensure that the best potential researchers are attracted into research careers;
2 to help universities to improve the quality of their research training and improve the employability of early stage researchers;
3 to improve retention of the best researchers by promoting better career development and management of research staff in research organisations.

At about the same time, The Concordat to Support the Career Development of Researchers (http:www.researchconcordat.ac.uk) was also launched, which adopted the principles of the European Charter for Researchers and Code of Conduct for the Recruitment of Researchers (2005). The Concordat presents a set of principles for the future support and management of research careers and under each principle, an explanation of how it may best be embedded into institutional practice.

At the time of writing, more than 100 organisations representing almost 1,000 institutions from 28 European and non-European countries have undersigned the Charter and Code principles. The European Commission, which gives its support to the implementation of the Charter and Code, has created the EURAXESS initiative (http://ec.europa.eu/euraxess/), which serves as an excellent resource for all researchers. The EURAXESS UK website, as an example, provides information and advice for international researchers who want to come to the UK and for those looking for jobs in research in Europe (http://www. euraxess.org.uk). EURAXESS Services is a network of more than 200 centres located around Europe and provides a free personalised service to help researchers and their families move in and around Europe as part of the European Union's strategy to stimulate employment and economic growth (http://ec.europa.eu/ euraxess/index.cfm/services/index).

Within the UK, Vitae has a great deal of information on career advice and has a link to the UK Research Staff Association which it supports (http://vitae. ac.uk/researchers/205761/UK-Research-Staff-Association.html). The latter was established in 2010 (the website is still under development) to provide a collective voice for researchers (although not just ECRs as PIs are included) at institutions across the UK.

Developments have also taken place at an institutional level. As well as Graduate School (or equivalent) provision, institutions are now often creating support specifically for ECRs. At the University of Sheffield, for example, we have a Researcher Development Team that works with ECRs to design, implement and evaluate a sustainable training programme for both academic and non-academic career pathways. One of the aims of the team is to hold a series of events requested by ECRs which will broaden researchers' awareness of future career opportunities within the UK and international academic fields, and other industries and sectors. Such events might include half-day workshops where outside specialists are invited to talk about a range of different career opportunities.

Similar developments have also taken place at Faculty level. Within the Faculty of Medicine, Dentistry and Health at the University of Sheffield, all new ECRs are given career planning assistance in a systematic manner (Figure 9.1) by the Medicine, Dentistry and Health Post-Doc Society, including provision of a Managing your Career workshop in addition to support of peers, PIs and mentors. A recommendation is that all new ECRs need to make a general career plan within the first year of the start of their contract, identifying his/her training needs and the skills required for success in their chosen career path.

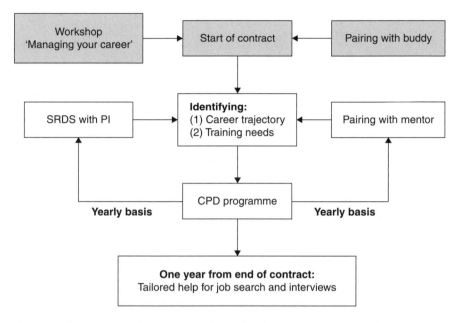

Figure 9.1 Career trajectory for postdoctoral researchers during their fixed-term contract. From Lee, Gowers, Ellis, *et al.* (2010), *International Journal for Researcher Development*, 1(4), p. 280, figure 3.

Note: SRDS = Staff Review and Development Scheme.

Which career?

Perhaps the majority of people in their first ECR appointment anticipate that their careers will develop along either a research and/or academic route. However, it is increasingly the case that fewer of these people will stay in higher education and that a significant proportion will take up non-academic careers (see also Chapter 1). Therefore, it is not only important for you to be aware of the range of non-academic careers that are available (Figure 9.2) but also to market a whole range of skills and competencies in addition to subject-specific skills. As Vitae (2009c) describe, such competencies may include:

- Understanding and experience of the generation of new knowledge at the forefront of their discipline.
- The ability to manage projects, resources and budgets.
- The ability to work as part of a team, to work alongside senior colleagues and to advise and train others including both staff and students.
- The ability to be proactive and to generate new business and consultancy work.

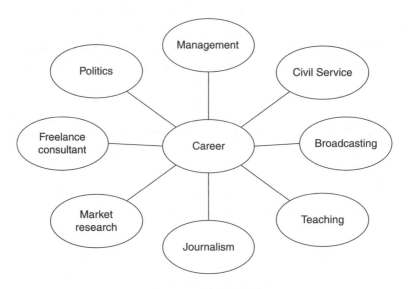

Figure 9.2 Examples of non-academic careers in Arts and Humanities.

- The ability to solve problems, show initiative and make decisions in both research and administrative settings.

One way of keeping abreast of career developments in one's field is to take note of information made available by Learned Societies. Often they provide relevant opportunities such as workshops to hear about developments at conferences. The latter are also particularly useful to acquaint oneself with PIs and ECRs from other institutions, to establish a more informal way of learning what opportunities might be available – in other words, networking. Will Kintish (www.kintish.co.uk), a leading authority on Networking Skills training in the UK, describes networking as 'word-of-mouth' marketing. Although many people do not like networking it is a desirable skill and fortunately, it is a process that can be greatly enhanced by attending seminars, conferences and workshops. You can prepare for these by rehearsing your 'elevator pitch' – the two-minute summary of your research that you would give to someone if you had only a few moments of their time. Think about what is interesting and distinctive about your research and practice, making it sound engaging to different kinds of audience, both specialist and non-specialist. You will then be ready to make connections with the people you meet – some of whom will be journal editors, funders, or potential future employers, and so well worth leaving with a good first impression of you and your work.

In the past, institutional careers offices seemed to be more focused on gradu-ates and postgraduates largely because they were by far the largest cohort in need of help. Moreover, before the Concordat on Contract Research Staff Career Management in 1996, there was little, if any, involvement of careers officers with

ECRs. Fortunately, times have now changed and often but not always, institutional careers offices now have specialist advisers for you. This development has been accelerated by the provision of funding which followed the Roberts Report (2002) but unfortunately will shortly end. It remains to be seen what effect this will have on specialist careers advice for ECRs. As an example of increased interest of ECRs seeking careers advice, at the University of Sheffield, consultations (which do not automatically equate to number of individuals) between ECRs and specialist careers advisers, increased fourfold between 2007 and 2009.

Careers advisers are a source of confidential and objective advice and are particularly useful as they maintain a good overview of the graduate labour market, the skills employers seek and how this will impact on job applications to organisations outside academia.

For individuals seeking career guidance, typically you will be asked to identify:

- your transferable skills that you could apply to other areas of employment;
- what interests you, what you find enjoyable and what puts you off;
- what values you have such as whether you would prefer the environment of a profit or non profit working sector;
- if you have any specific constraints such as family commitments or are tied to a geographical location.

With this information, careers advisers will then try to help explore suitable options. The availability of different careers will be highlighted together with discussions of potential employers and vacancies.

The next stage will be the application process where various types of support, including one-to-one, booklets and podcasts, are offered such as advice on presentation of a CV, how to complete online competency-based application forms (Table 9.1), which are often used by large corporate employers, and application forms that may be used by the public sector which match skills and achievements with the person specification required.

Table 9.1 Examples of typical questions from a competency-based application form

---

Outline a time when you have put in additional effort or 'gone the extra mile' in order to achieve results.

What motivated you to put in additional effort and how did you ensure that you produced a good result?

Describe an occasion when you have had to work with others to achieve a goal.

What did you do to help the team work well together?

What were the challenges or obstacles you had to overcome?

Tell us about a time when you have had to overcome a disappointment or setback.

Describe a time when you have provided excellent customer service.

If the application is successful, then support is offered at the interview stage which includes one-to-one interviews, use of audio-visual material on the campus TV network, online talks and podcasts. At some institutions, computer software called 'Interviewer' may be used where users can choose the interview scenario and after questioning, they are given time to produce their own answers which can then be compared to what the respective employer might be looking for. As is often the case for ECRs, this may be your first experience of an employment interview; so if required, it is possible for you to have several sessions with the careers adviser to gain important practical experience of interviewing.

Group activities have also expanded in recent years and careers advisers lead workshops on career planning, job applications and interview sessions. Other topics may also be delivered on a one-off basis. Careers advisers may also organise skills development sessions with major employers on such topics as time management, leadership, commercial awareness and negotiation skills.

Even if you are unable to visit the Careers Office, many institutions will offer an E guidance service which offers online support and possible CV checks. The Vitae website (http://www.vitae.ac.uk) is also able to offer careers information and has links to the Graduate Prospects website (http://www.prospects.ac.uk) and to the ACGAS online careers support package called University Researchers and the Job Market (http://www.acgas.org.uk/agcas_resources/115-University-Researchers-and-the-Job-Market).

At an individual level, workshops may be provided by staff (not just careers advisers) at institutions to try to assist how you can best develop yourself and to make use of the support offered by the institution. Such a workshop might include completion of a Myers–Briggs Type Indicator (MBTI) questionnaire beforehand which can be used to help you understand your strengths and consider areas for development. The MBTI assessment is a psychometric questionnaire designed to measure psychological preferences and is the world's most widely used personality assessment. In addition to the MBTI, alternatives include the Margerison–McCann Team Management Profile (TMS Development International Ltd), OPQ32r (SHL Group Ltd) and Strength Deployment Inventory (Personal Strengths Publishing, Inc). These are all development tools to increase self awareness and to allow employees to identify their strengths and development areas, which in addition to improving working practice can also be used to help you market yourself to potential employers. These tools can be offered by careers advisers or Independent Consultants (usually at a cost) and can also be used by employers as an aid to help identify an employee's preferences but not skills. An easy introduction to these development tools would be to use the Strength Deployment Inventory due to its lower cost and ease of use. Once these tools have been completed, a hard copy report is usually given to the user which reflects their preferences. Outcomes from these tools are often presented diagrammatically such as The Margerison–McCann Team Management Wheel as used in the Team Management Profile (Figure 9.3).

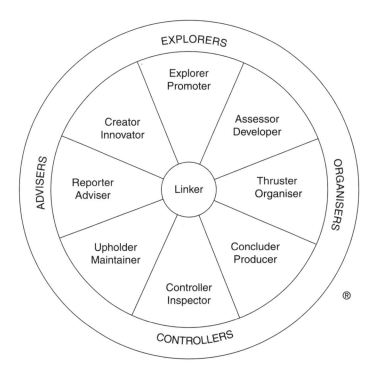

Figure 9.3 The Margerison–McCann Team Management Wheel ®.

Reproduced by kind permission of TMS Development International, 2011 (www.tmsdi.com)

The application

If you have got this far on the road to making a formal application, we assume that you have already done some research on the position in question, such as who you will be working with, the quality of the institution and the exact details of the post. If not, then we strongly encourage you to do so before going forward. So the next step presumably is to create the most appropriate CV for the post. This is perhaps more difficult than what it initially seems and it is certainly not appropriate to think that a typical academic-like CV is going to be right for every type of post that you apply for. Table 9.2 clearly illustrates the different emphases that should be put in CVs depending on where the post is. For example, if the post is non-academic then presumably it would be better to emphasise the relevant transferable skills that you have learnt which are appropriate for the post, rather than concentrating on research publications. Vitae give good advice about producing such a skills-based CV (http://vitae.ac.uk/researchers/1375/Skills-based-CVs.html).

Table 9.2 Differing emphases in three types of CV

Academic CV	Industrial CV	Non-academic CV
Research reputation – publications, etc.	Admin experience – particularly management	Knowledge of the area/ commercial awareness
Teaching experience – lecturing, tutoring, mentoring	Research experience – relevant publications	Transferable ('soft') skills – communication, teamwork, etc.
Admin experience – organising, managing	Technical skills (subject specific)	Admin experience – organising, managing
Ability to attract funds	Transferable ('soft') skills	Numeracy
Technical skills (subject specific)	Commercial awareness	Reasons for changing career

Note: From AGCAS (www.agcas.org.uk) *University researchers and the job market: A practical career development resource for research staff* (p. 58).

A more typical academic CV might include the following:

- Name and contact details.
- Degree qualifications and dates when obtained.
- Positions held with dates and addresses.
- Any awards, prizes, honours including postdoctoral fellowships.
- Sources of any funding.
- Publications including books, book chapters, refereed journals, non-refereed publications, and finally abstracts and letters to the editor (typically in that order).
- Invited lectures and/or conference presentations.
- Teaching experience including any supervision experience.
- Any other information of relevance such as journal responsibilities, industrial collaboration, society positions, theses examined, etc.
- Referees including names, titles and contact information.

Of course any CV needs to be succinct, accurate and up-to-date and it is worth finding out before submitting a CV what is required from any particular institution, as often priorities and formats may differ.

As well as submitting your CV, it is usual that a cover letter accompanies it. The purpose of the letter is to state what position is being applied for, a brief description of why you are applying for the post (in other words why you are interested), a brief description of your relevant background and experience, highlighting major achievements and any other significant facts about yourself, which stresses why you are such a wonderful applicant (bearing in mind that you don't want to go over the top but on the other hand, the position may well be very competitive).

The interview

Once the application has been considered, usually a short-listing process takes place to decide who to ask for a formal interview. There is no doubt that in this situation you cannot hide behind your CV and you will be put on the spot to create a good impression. Although it may be said that an interview is not good in predicting later performance (Keats 2000: 86), it can show how well the interviewee can fit into the organisation. In this case, personal impressions will be used including what the interviewers make of the interviewee's behaviour; first impressions seem to be a powerful influence as decisions on the post are often made in the first few minutes of the interview. It appears that impressions are more favourable when the interviewee is most like the interviewer (Keats 2000: 87). So we recommend that dress is professional and appropriate for the position.

Possible types of questions in an interview (more so for non-academic posts) include the following:

- *Behavioural* – these are based on the detailed person specification of the job or a general statement of key competencies that the organisation expects its employees to have e.g. 'Can you tell us of your experience and achievements in working with others in successful management projects?'
- *Personality* – these gain an insight into your personality and attitudes e.g. 'How would you handle a very demanding customer from a company which has a multi-million pound contract with the firm?'
- *Career* – these test an understanding of the job and reasons for applying e.g. 'Why have you applied for this management position with such a strong research background?'
- *Hypothetical* – they can test your understanding of the job or more generally how good you are at thinking on your feet e.g. 'How would you get urgent reports out if the computer system goes down?'
- *Knowledge-based* – these test your knowledge of the organisation and to see how well you have done your homework e.g. 'Give a brief description of your understanding of the overall management structure of the organisation.'

As well as finding out aspects of the position and the institution, it is probably a good idea to do some background work on members of the interview panel to prepare you for what they might ask questions on.

Another key point to consider is that most institutions now want applicants to give a formal research presentation as part of the selection process. This will often be for 30–60 minutes and it is crucial that all aspects of the presentation are correct. Therefore, it is important to know who will be in the audience and what they want from the presentation, such as research plans, so that you give them what they really want. This is certainly not the time to run 10 minutes late and leave no time for questions or to make slide information so small that it can't be seen without a telescope. It's always a good idea not only to run through your talk a few times to yourself beforehand but to ask colleagues to sit in and make helpful suggestions. Unless you have already sent your presentation online, it is probably a good idea to take two different formats of the presentation with you, as it is not the first time that a memory stick and/or CD have failed. If you can, try to give yourself time to acquaint yourself with the room where you will give your talk as this should make you feel less stressed and hopefully more comfortable.

Either before and/or after the talk you will probably have less formal discussions with potential colleagues from within and outside the department. This is always a good opportunity to get a feeling about the place and whether you think you will be able to fit in. It is also good to see whether there are any possibilities for any collaborative work. Whilst the process may be informal, say a talk over coffee or lunch, your potential colleagues are also gathering information about you to feedback into the selection process e.g. how well do they think you would fit in the organisation. It is therefore important to remain professional.

Following the interview you will probably be asked to meet the Chair of the Interview Panel. You may even be asked if you are willing to take the position should it be offered. Depending on whether the position was offered or not, it is the right time to let the Chair know whether you are still interested in the position should it be offered to you. Don't forget, even if you are not the first or even the second choice, you may still be offered the position as candidates often decide they don't want the job and/or accept a position elsewhere. So the message is, try to be positive at all times, that way you give yourself the best chance.

Finally, if you have been offered the position, great, but don't get too carried away as this may be the only opportunity to confirm and/or amend the terms and conditions of the contract of employment. Apart from one's own personal financial agreement, you might want to have put in writing the promise of, for example, a special piece of equipment or the details of the start-up fund if you are lucky enough to have one.

Applying for promotion

As this book is written for ECRs, the main emphasis is more on career planning and obtaining a position. However, for those who continue in academia, who are primarily research active and who are more likely to be high-flyers, there could still be the possibility of promotion early on. For a junior academic who has been very successful in obtaining grants, fellowships and publications in high-quality journals, it could still be difficult to know whether they are at an appropriate stage to apply for promotion. If possible, discussions with senior colleagues including the Head of Department would be important not only for their judgement and advice as to whether the timing is right but also to gain their support. If the support is forthcoming, applications for promotion usually take place on an annual basis and clear guidelines are given as to the format of the CV and any supporting statements and the timescale of events, as the application passes through the university committees. A word of caution though, not every case is approved no matter how good they may be, so be prepared for possible disappointment. However, it is always useful to ask for feedback on why the application for promotion was rejected, as it can help improve for next time as well as giving clear objectives to focus on. Sometimes applications can be made two or three times before they are eventually approved. One strategy that sometimes works is to obtain a senior position at another institution. This then puts the employing institution on the spot because they know that you might go elsewhere unless they can make you a similar or better offer. However, it can backfire as the employing institution might still not offer promotion in which case, a potentially difficult decision needs to be made as to whether to leave for promotion or to remain where you are.

Commercializing your research

Academics and industrialists are often thought to be poles apart, as portrayed in the early chapters of David Lodge's novel *Nice Work* (1988). However, more and more scholars are foraging into the world of commercial exploitation. You may find that your research skills or inventions are valuable in the world outside of the ivory towered quad. You could have the basis of a business of some sort, a development which successive governments seem increasingly keen to promote. Most universities have spawned 'spin-off' companies and many now boast a technology, or bio-incubator, usually a building or possibly a small industrial estate, housing emerging high-tech businesses whose roots have grown out of academic departments.

So how do you go about commercializing your research, what are the advantages and disadvantages? Possibly the simplest introduction to commercial activity is to do some form of consultancy for remuneration. Most institutions are happy for their academic staff to do this sort of outside work. It shows the value of academic research to a wider society, improves profile and can lead to more substantive and lucrative contract research if you do a good job. However, some institutions only allow academic staff to partake in consultancy activities and even though in exceptional cases, you may be allowed to for the benefit of the institution, you may not receive any payment. So depending on your employer's policy and your contract, payments may end up in your bank account or be used to bolster your research funding depending on how you go about it. You would be well advised to go through your institution's commercial liaison office and certainly seek their permission before agreeing to any such work. Your employer will usually arrange for your consultancy work to be covered by some form of liability insurance in return for retaining a (hopefully) small portion of the fee.

Your employer may allow you to do your own independent consultancy work but obviously you will not then have the benefit of their professional liability insurance. The range of payments for consultancy work is amazingly broad and varied. Obviously, the more specialist and directly applicable your advice, the more valuable it may be to your client. As a very rough guide, you might expect to receive somewhere in the region of one week's salary (or more) for every full day of consultancy plus full reimbursement of all expenses. Do not underestimate any time spent on preparation and writing written reports. Make sure you agree your pricings with the client in advance (or at least get their written agreement to an estimate) and be certain to have obtained reliable legal and tax advice beforehand. This is where your institution's commercial liaison office (or equivalent administrative office) should be able to save you from embarrassing conversations about value added tax, state taxes, etc!

Maybe you have grander ideas to get really rich, a new way of making shopping trolleys or self-sealing beer cans? Perhaps you should start a company. Several successful companies have emerged or 'spun out' of academic institutions. Setting up a spin-out is not something to be done lightly. It is a major commitment of your time, usually ends in commercial failure and is certainly likely to be stressful and push your people skills to the limit! So why bother at all? Well, you could get rich (but this is statistically highly unlikely), you may be able to fund a project that would otherwise never leave the drawing board and you will certainly gain new and valuable experience of the commercial sector. Some projects lend themselves to commercial exploitation, rather than funding via the classical grant application route to charitable or government-funded research councils. For example, your idea may be considered too narrow or not high-tech enough to gain traditional grant funding, or it may be in an area outside of the main funders' remits. Again, before you start it is important to check your contractual position. Most universities encourage this type of activity, but not unreasonably, they will expect to get their share of emerging intellectual property (IP) and commercial development.

So who is likely to fund your new spin-out? Assuming that you are not independently wealthy and are unwilling to mortgage your house, then you are going to need some sort of investment to make your company fly. There are a range of potential sources, from (possibly) local university funds for pump priming, local/regional business development loans, venture capital funding, and so-called 'business angels'. In addition, many big pharmaceutical companies (and those in other sectors) have their own 'venture capital' arms that invest in areas very close to their own interests. The one thing that all these sources of funding have in common is that you will have to give away a share of your company in return for their investment. This can be a very tricky balancing act. At inception, you may feel you own 100% of the idea but then essentially you have a hundred percent of nothing. Your holding may come down substantially depending upon your institution's policies to IP related to your work. You will need to sell off even more to lure in an appropriate investor. Before you head off into venture capital land you will need to make sure you have solid IP in place, again your institution should be able to help with this most important aspect.

To make a spin-out work you need to appeal to the basic human instinct of greed. Your investor needs to be convinced that by giving your company £200,000 they have a chance of getting it back tenfold over in 2–3 years. You need a sound idea, one that can be protected from being copied somehow (patents, copyright) and is a guaranteed money-spinning idea. Most of all you need to really do your homework regarding how your idea can be turned into something that should make money in the real world. You will also need to persuade the investor to invest in you. You (and your IP) are the unique selling point. They want to see passion, commitment (they like to see you taking a risk with your money too if you can manage it) and, above all, they need to be convinced that you and your plan will deliver massive returns, otherwise, they would simply put their money somewhere else because they are by definition, not the sort to be happy with the returns they would get from the FTSE100.

Equity issues

In 1996, the UK Research Councils together with the Committee of Vice-Chancellors and Principals (CVCP, now Universities UK) together with other bodies signed a 'Concordat on Contract Research Staff Career Management' (now updated by The Concordat to Support the Career Development of Researchers – see above). This was an important step as it set standards for the career management and conditions of employment of researchers employed by higher education institutions on fixed-term or similar contracts. It has since been used as a general reference point for good practice across the UK higher education sector. Since then, The Fixed Term Employees (Prevention of Less Favourable Treatment) Regulations 2002 have come into force. These Regulations stated that fixed-term employees should not be treated less favourably than comparable permanent employees. Amongst other recommendations, universities have to conduct a four-year review such that all staff with four or more years' continuous service on successive fixed-term contracts must be considered for transfer onto an open ended contract. Although the open ended contract is not guaranteed, it does mean that some of you do not have to keep on working with fixed-term contracts.

Recently, in the UK there have been some significant changes regarding recruitment and selection. In October 2010, the Equality Act came into force and aims to provide a simpler, more consistent and more effective legal framework for preventing discrimination. This act replaced the following equality legislation:

- The Equal Pay Act 1970
- The Sex Discrimination Act 1975
- The Race Relations Act 1976
- The Disability Discrimination Act 199
- The Employment Equality (Religion or Belief) Regulations 2003
- The Employment Equality (Sexual Orientation) Regulations 2003
- The Employment Equality (Age) Regulations 2006
- The Equality Act 2006, Part 2
- The Equality Act (Sexual Orientation) Regulations 2007.

To protect against discrimination, victimisation and harassment it is suggested that the new Equality Act be consulted.

Interestingly, a recent report which examined the characteristics of postdoctoral career trajectories concluded that females were more likely to be unavailable for employment on fixed-term or on part-time contracts, which raises an issue as to whether gender differences are more apparent in research career progression following completion of the doctorate (Crossouard 2010). Similarly, a report from the USA showed that despite significant increases in participation rates of females in doctoral programmes, when it comes to the filling of senior positions, a much smaller percentage of females are appointed (Mason and Goulden 2003). When data were examined it became apparent that women with early babies (defined as one who joins the household at any point up to 5 years after his or her parent completes a PhD) leave academia before obtaining their first tenure track job. A further conclusion of the study was that 'married with children' is the success formula for men but the opposite for women. Of course, not all women want to pursue a tenure track academic career, but those that do will need to make some serious decisions about marriage, having a family and if and when to have children. With this in mind, the University of California has devised a Faculty Family Friendly Initiative which amongst other ideas, proposes a flexible part-time option for faculty with substantial family responsibilities, a guarantee to make high-quality child care slots available to faculty and re-entry postdoctoral fellowships to encourage parents who have taken time off to return to their institution.

It is clear that much needs to be done to ensure gender equity in both professional and family goals for future generations of academics.

Top tips for developing your career

- Consider a career plan as early as is possible.
- Be aware of institutional, national and international bodies that support the development of ECR careers.
- Remember that only a minority of ECRs take up academic posts and that a career outside academia is more likely.
- Seek out specialist career advisers at your institution who focus on the needs of ECRs.
- Learn how to construct the most appropriate CV and how to prepare for a job interview.
- Have an awareness of employment contracts and the legal framework which supports them.

Scenario 9.1 – When networking made all the difference

An academic position had been advertised and both Lorna and Gillian were very strong contenders as their research background was directly related to the vacant post. Lorna knew about the post well before it was formally advertised as she had been told about it by some ECRs she had met at a conference, who were working in the same department as that advertising the post. At that stage she had also found out who the Head of Department (HoD) was who was wanting a junior academic and realised that she had known him from a previous meeting, where she had given a conference paper. Yes, she certainly remembered him as they had also spent an interesting afternoon together with other colleagues on a conference outing.

Informally, Lorna contacted the HoD and in their conversation, she indicated to him that she was very interested in the post, would like to come and visit the department as soon as was possible and would almost certainly put in an application. After Lorna had submitted her application and was invited for an interview, she felt confident about the post she had applied for, she already knew quite a lot about the institution and the HoD and she considered she was as well prepared as she could be. In contrast, Gillian had also applied for the post after she had seen it advertised. Of course, she had heard of the HoD's reputation and knew a little about the institution, but otherwise she had no prior contact with the HoD or his existing ECRs as she was more interested in producing high-quality publications than being seen at conferences. When it came to the interview, both Lorna and Gillian performed well but on balance Lorna was offered the post which she readily accepted.

So, despite Gillian being the stronger candidate on paper as she had slightly better-quality publications than Lorna, she was not offered the job. This could be due to a number of factors that might include the fact that Lorna was already known to the HoD and to the department, they had met previously in both pleasing and sociable circumstances, and the HoD was impressed by how keen Lorna was about the job. In contrast, Gillian did not seem to come across as quite as friendly, possibly due to that fact that she had never previously met the HoD. The fact is, that probably made all the difference.

Scenario 9.2 – When you just get the feeling that you are banging your head against a brick wall

Ali was now in his third ECR position and was approaching his 30th birthday. It hadn't gone quite as he had planned as he thought by now he might have got the academic post he had so badly wanted. However, over the last couple of years he had failed to get any of the several positions he had applied for, and his future was becoming problematic as his current ECR post was coming to an end and he was not happy about trying to apply for another one, as he needed some stability in his life now that he was to get married and hopefully buy a house. It had been a despairing time for him and he had many discussions with his colleagues and his future wife about what he should do next.

Reluctantly, he decided that he would have to consult the institution's career adviser and explain his situation. Ali's story came as no real surprise to the adviser who over the last few years had seen an increasing number of ECRs in the same position of not being able to get the academic post they had wanted. In discussions with Ali, the adviser realised that he had an interest and expertise in project management especially with budgets and he suggested to Ali that maybe he should consider working in the financial sector. At first Ali was reluctant to take this seriously as he was an experienced researcher and thought it would be wasting his previous experience and talents. However, after re-considering the possibilities, especially with regards to specialist areas in accountancy where his previous knowledge and research expertise would be an advantage, he began to warm to the idea. Yes, he realised that he would have to carry on studying for a few years more and take professional exams, but at least at the end of the training he would be much better placed to pursue a secure career rather than facing the insecurities of being a researcher.

Summary

It is vital that early and thorough career planning is a high priority, with institutional postdoctoral societies now playing an important role. As well as making use of local careers officers, there are many new websites on careers that provide much relevant information. It is important that you are aware of how best to make a job application as well as having knowledge of what may be required at interview. Also, an understanding of equity issues is becoming increasingly more relevant to careers.

Recommended/Further reading

Blaxter, L., Hughes, C. and Tight, M. (1998) *The academic career handbook.* Buckingham,UK: Open University Press.
This text has an emphasis on supporting staff development and primarily offers guidance on networking, teaching, researching, writing and managing. It is designed for those working or hoping to work within the higher education system.

Ali, L. and Graham, B. (2000) *Moving on in your career: A guide for academics and postgraduates.* London: Routledge.
This book shows researchers what is required to make a continuing career in academia and has a special focus on the skills acquired through academic research and how to use them to pursue a wide variety of career options.

Grant, W. and Sherrington, P. (2006) *Managing your academic career (universities into the 21st century)*. Basingstoke, UK: Palgrave Macmillan.
This book provides new academic staff in the humanities and social sciences with a guide to success in their chosen career. It includes how to get a job, time management, relations with colleagues, effective teaching, PhD supervision and examining, getting published and career development.

Miller V. J. and Furlong, J. S. (2008) *The academic job search handbook*. Philadelphia, PA: University of Pennsylvania Press.
This text includes information on aspects of the academic job search that are common to all levels with invaluable tips for those seeking their first or second academic position. There is also a chapter on alternatives to academic jobs.

Chapter 10

Conclusions and future directions

Over the last few years there have been some significant developments to enhance the experience of ECRs such as the introduction of local and national postdoctoral associations. However, in the UK particularly, many changes are taking place both inside and outside of higher education, and in this chapter we will discuss how these changes may impact upon you and future ECRs. We consider the undeniable decrease in opportunities to enter academia necessitates greater emphasis on strategies for developing researcher employability skills to help you and your fellow ECRs to explore alternative job markets. On the positive side, we review the efforts being made by national bodies to make proposals and recommendations to try and enhance the experience and profile of ECRs.

During your time as an ECR, we hope that you will have benefited from some of the recent improvements to national strategies in the UK by 'Roberts Funding' and by the activities of Vitae, which have greatly enhanced the overall experience of ECRs. Similarly, the National Postdoctoral Association and EURODOC in the USA and Europe respectively have also raised the profile of ECRs. These activities have led to the introduction of two specific journals, *International Journal for Researcher Development* and *Journal of Postdoctoral Affairs* which also demonstrate an increasing interest in research studies in the field.

However, in the UK there are some worrying developments. Firstly, 'Roberts Funding' will cease in 2012 and at the time of writing HEIs are presently exploring how to sustain their support for ECRs as well as postgraduate researchers. One option is to recover ring-fenced funding to support this including from PhD fees and from new successfully awarded research grants that include the appointment of research staff. HEIs are currently trying to decide which ECR activities can be supported, and then, to achieve their delivery, how to calculate the costs. Any significant overall reduction in funding would be unfortunate as many of the advances in ECR development and provision, such as the funding of local postdoctoral societies, have originated from Roberts funding. As an ECR, you may have an important role to play in evaluating and responding to the provision currently made in your institution, which could help research leaders in making decisions about how to prioritise funding and support.

Second, there has been a general and continuing reduction in university funding by central government with significant changes predicted for future funding. We do not know what effects these changes will have on student numbers, including postgraduate researchers, and the workload of academic staff. These factors may influence decisions about pursuing academic careers, as well as declining pay, working conditions and pensions, and an increase in administrative burdens and bureaucracy. Unfortunately, many of these factors have become negative influences. These are worrying times for all academics, but especially for those ECRs who have their hopes set on a career in academia, since for the present at least, traditional academic posts are in short supply.

However, as Partridge (2011) notes, anyone with a doctorate has skills they can take elsewhere. Skills such as academic writing, knowledge of foreign languages, the ability to carry out research and meet long-term goals, are very much sought after in industries which include banking, advertising, publishing and law. You will be a desirable prospect to many future employers, and so it is worth looking outside academia for other possibilities, especially in the short term. A concern we have though, is that many academics as line managers have the mistaken belief that ECRs will more likely get an academic position when they leave their employment. Somehow academics must be made aware that this is far from the truth; and in doing so, this will raise the importance, need and support for researcher development. Again, you can play a part in this, both by speaking to your own mentor about career prospects, and by contributing to local and national discussions about the need for a diversification in ECR support.

A third factor for academic careers in the UK in particular, is that the Default Retirement Age was phased out in October 2011, which now means that employers will be no longer be allowed to dismiss staff just because they have reached the age of 65. Together with a rise in the state pension age for both men and women, it will no doubt mean that academic staff will work longer and retire later which could impact on academic job vacancies and overall staff turnover. This will also raise the age profile for academic staff, which has been increasing not only in the UK but also in Canada and Australia (Universities UK 2007). All of these factors should re-emphasise the need for ECRs to develop employability skills for non-academic careers.

Developing employability skills in Sheffield

At the University of Sheffield, in early 2011, in order to understand the training needs of ECRs, two questionnaires were created. One was completed by ECRs ($n = 29$) who wished to pursue an academic career and the other was completed by those ECRs ($n = 26$) who were primarily seeking an alternative career. In requests for workshops by those pursuing an academic career, the most popular request was on grant writing, with specific guidance on style, structure and when to include pilot data. The second most requested workshop was on where to apply for grants.

When ECRs who were seeking alternative careers were specifically asked about their skills and knowledge, deficiencies were noted in the following topics:

- A good understanding of possible career options outside academia that reflects my professional expertise and talents.
- A good understanding of what employers want and what skills are required in careers of interest to me outside academia.
- A knowledge of how to articulate and market my research and transferable skills on a CV and in job applications.
- A commercial awareness and understanding of the market sector and company/public sector roles outside academia.
- A knowledge of what is expected at a job interview and feeling confident about articulating my skills in person.

Although we realise that the size of the above cohorts are small, a number of specific training needs have been highlighted which would be worth pursuing. It would also be worthwhile repeating such a training needs analysis in larger cohorts and in other institutions so that targeted career development programmes can be initiated.

New recommendations (including training)

As you evaluate the provision and support that has been made available to you as an ECR, you might like to set your experience in the context of a recent report that commented on the review of progress in implementing the recommendations made by Sir Gareth Roberts (Research Councils UK 2010). Of particular relevance are three recommendations:

- *Recommendation 2* – Research Councils UK needs to ensure that specific funding and other initiatives continue to stimulate and reinforce the development of transferable skills and support for career development of researchers, using mechanisms that are efficient for the whole higher education sector and other stakeholders.
- *Recommendation 3* – All funders must contribute financially (directly and indirectly) to the skills and career development of PhD students and research staff.
- *Recommendation 4* – Research organisations must ensure that expertise is maintained in specialist roles dedicated to maintaining the skills development and support for career development of researchers, even following changes in funding mechanisms.

From these recommendations there is certainly the realisation that much has been gained and that these gains should be maintained by using different funding streams wherever possible.

From a more practical point of view, in the UK, Vitae have introduced the Researcher Development Framework (RDF), which we have already mentioned in Chapter 1. The RDF represents a major new approach to researcher development and can be used as a tool for planning, promoting and supporting the personal, professional and career development of researchers as outlined in Figure 10.1.

A problem that we have mentioned before has been the inability of institutions to recognise and support ECR positions, unlike the structure that exists for students and academics. However, in the USA as far back as 2000, The National Academy of Sciences proposed a number of action points including point 2, in which institutions should 'Develop distinct policies and standards for postdocs, modeled on those available for graduate students and faculty' (The National Academy of Sciences 2000). In general we support this proposal and would suggest that a Code of Practice for ECRs is considered by the Quality Assurance

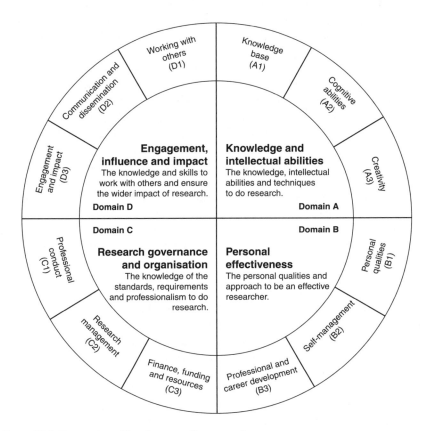

Figure 10.1 Researchers Development Framework.

Vitae®, © 2010 Careers Research and Advisory Centre (CRAC) Limited. www.vitae.ac.uk/RDFconditionsofuse.

Agency (QAA 2004) of the UK similar to what has already been produced for PhD students. Among other issues, this Code would be able to address working conditions and include recommendations for handling grievances and irreconcilable differences which can be a major problem (Ferber 1999); it could also include training.

As we discussed, ECRs are keen to learn a whole range of employability skills and it is important that line managers and institutions recognise that resources be put in place to enable it to happen. A recent report (Fonseca-Kelly, Operario, Finger, *et al.* 2010) has made clear that in science, 'postdocs who gauge their success solely on bench productivity do so at their own professional peril'. Moreover, 'Postdocs reporting the greatest amount of structured oversight and formal training are much more likely to say they are satisfied, to give their advisers high ratings, to experience relatively few conflicts with their advisers and to be more productive in terms of numbers of publications compared with those with the least oversight and training' (Davis 2005: 11). Similarly, a more recent finding in the UK found that well-rounded ECRs with initiative, who are not always 'tied to the bench' are more successful academically (Lee, Gowers, Ellis, *et al.* 2010). The ECRs who featured in our chapters on writing and teaching would no doubt be the first to say that a consideration of career development and future training needs is yet another demand on your time, but the evidence shows that this extra investment in preparing your CV and demonstrating your transferable skills could help to set you apart from others in your cohort when it comes to finding employment.

Further reinforcement of the need to provide more training opportunities for ECRs has come from a focus group that was formed from attendees at a conference in the USA (*The Scientist* 2006). One of their ten recommendations was:

> Offer at the institutional or program level, courses and workshops for post-docs to enhance professional development skills, including public speaking and presentation skills, grantsmanship and scientific writing, interviewing and negotiating skills, laboratory management, and mentoring skills, as well as responsible conduct of science.

Although we have focused on the need for ECRs to develop their employability skills, a recent development in the USA has been the introduction of teaching postdoctoral fellowships. These fellowships have become more popular as a way for ECRs who particularly want to enter academia to make themselves more competitive. In these programmes, ECRs learn about course design and classroom and lab management; they also mentor undergraduates. Some of these posts are beginning to emerge in the UK, and as with all academic vacancies, it is worth keeping yourself fully informed of opportunities by signing up to the job notification lists of websites like www.jobs.ac.uk, where most posts are now advertised.

As a postdoc survey by Sigma Xi in the USA (Sigma Xi Postdoc Survey 2005) showed that almost two thirds of science postdocs have received no training on how to teach, institutions are now addressing this issue by providing programmes that support teaching and mentoring at the postdoctoral level. For example, at the University of Sheffield, a new programme called the Sheffield Teaching Assistant has been introduced to help ECRs develop their teaching. The programme consists of four themes which include: teaching large groups, teaching small groups, assessment and feedback, and supervising research projects. A certificate is awarded on completion of the programme.

Messages for ECRs and their colleagues

Throughout this book we have highlighted the skills and strategies that ECRs need in order to function effectively, maintain motivation and wellbeing, and progress towards future employment, whether in academia or beyond. We finish with some recommendations for you, your fellow ECRs and your mentors – and we hope that you will benefit from discussing these with your colleagues and considering how they apply to your own situation.

In our discussions with ECRs during the writing of this book we have met individuals who are resilient and resourceful in dealing with the often challenging circumstances of an ECR, and in particular with the uncertainty over their future – exacerbated by the factors mentioned in this chapter. They have talked about the ways in which the demands of 'early career' do not always form a natural stepping stone to success in 'mid career', often being dependent on the support and generosity of a mentor who has concern for their ECRs' futures. In the regrettably hierarchical world of academia, ECRs sometimes feel that they have limited control over their own careers: putting substantial effort into joint publications and team research projects, for instance, might limit their opportunities to publish their own doctoral work, or to gain teaching experience – giving them a narrow profile of skills for which they might then be criticised in future lectureship applications. Mentors, therefore, have a responsibility to ensure that their ECRs are on a career pathway, not a cul de sac.

Scenario 10.1 – Is my CV good enough?

Dan is nearing the end of a postdoc research fellowship and beginning to think about careers in academia. His publications are mainly archaeological reports – the detailed accounts of the sites he has been working on during his postdoc – and he is aware that he needs more peer-reviewed publications to make him attractive to a department concerned about its Research Excellence Framework (REF) submission. Likewise, he has taught only a few guest lectures on modules, having sought opportunities to gain teaching experience, whilst being aware that his obligations to his funding body mean that he should not devote too much of his paid time to teaching preparation and delivery. He is embarrassed about how to describe his teaching potential on his CV, feeling that his lack of experience does not reflect his willingness to engage with that aspect of academic life. Having been a successful 'early career' researcher, the path to 'mid career' is by no means clear and he is now considering leaving academia altogether.

Where ECRs are successful and happy in their work, they often cite the presence of an inspiring senior researcher, who despite a busy schedule makes time to read drafts of papers or grant applications, and who is generous in allowing the junior researcher to build an independent reputation rather than bolstering that of their mentor. ECRs perhaps need better training in realising the potential career limitations of joint authorship, short-term fellowships and so on – and mentors in recognising their responsibility to support junior colleagues into successful, independent positions. Clarifying expectations at the outset of a research contract can be helpful for both parties, with questions including 'will I be allowed time to publish my doctoral work or pursue new projects?' and 'what is the department's policy on author ordering in joint papers – and is this one that will be widely understood by readers in the discipline?'

Scenario 10.2 – A moment of fame

While working on a physics project on polymer alloys, Jon had a breakthrough, discovering a new way of creating colours on banknotes that could make them resistant to fraud. His discovery was promoted by the university's media centre and reported in a national newspaper, as well as contributing to publications in prestigious scientific journals. Jon asked his supervisor, the primary investigator on the research grant, if he would like to share the credit for the research, since it was carried out 'on his payroll'. He was gratified by his PI's decision to turn down this offer, allowing Jon to enjoy the moment of fame in his own right, and so bolstering his future career opportunities by clearly giving him credit for the research. Jon's discovery still reflected well on his PI's project and would be reported back to the funding body as a team effort, but the senior researcher's decision not to share the glory was a supportive one that could have far-reaching benefits for Jon's career.

ECRs need to be given the opportunity to decide whether a career in academia is for them – and mentors to understand whether that is the ECR's aim or not. If it is, well-supported opportunities for teaching experience will be needed – and not those that involve providing last-minute cover for a first year lecture to hundreds of students, but rather those that allow an ECR to plan carefully, develop a good relationship with a group of students, and receive constructive feedback on the style and content of their teaching. Negative first experiences of teaching could have a damaging effect on ECRs' career intentions, perhaps depriving academia of a potentially stellar lecturer by plunging them too far into the deep end.

Summary

It seems clear therefore, that ECRs know what they want in terms of training provision by institutions. It is now up to the policy makers to make sure that it happens.

Recommended/Further reading

http://www.vitae.ac.uk/researchers/428241/Researcher-Development-Framework. html
The Researcher Development Framework (RDF) website explains what the RDF is, who it is for and how researchers can make the most of it.

References

Acas. (2010) *Bullying and harassment at work: A guide for managers and employees.* London: Advisory, Conciliation and Arbitration Service.

Akerlind, G. S. (2005) Postdoctoral researchers: Roles, function and career prospects. *Higher Education Research and Development,* 24(1): 21–40.

Akerlind, G. S. (2009) Postdoctoral research positions as preparation for an academic career. *International Journal for Researcher Development,* 1(1): 84–96.

Bazeley, P. (2003) Defining 'early career' in research. *Higher Education,* 45(3): 257–279.

Becker, H. (1986) *Writing for social scientists: How to start and finish your thesis, book or article.* Chicago, IL: University of Chicago Press.

Bett, W. R. (1952) *The preparation and writing of medical papers for publication.* London: Menley and James.

Bettmann, M. (2009) Choosing a research project and a research mentor. *Circulation,* 119(13): 1832–1835.

Biggs, J. and Tang, C. (2007) *Teaching for quality learning at university* (3rd ed.). Maidenhead, UK: SRHE and Open University Press.

Boice, R. (1997). Strategies for enhancing scholarly productivity. In J. M. Moxley and T. Taylor (Eds), *Writing and publishing for academic authors* (2nd ed., pp. 19–34). Lanham, MD: Rowman & Littlefield.

Bonello, C. and Scaife, J. A. (2009) PEOR: Engaging students in demonstrations. *Journal of Science and Mathematics Education in Southeast Asia,* 32(1): 62–84.

Bradley, G. (2002) A really useful link between teaching and research. *Teaching in Higher Education* 7(4): 443–455.

Brande, D. (1983) *Becoming a writer.* London: Macmillan. (Original work published 1934.)

Bransford, J. D., Brown, A. L., and Cocking, R. R. (Eds). (2000) *How people learn: Brain, mind, experience, and school* (expanded ed.). Washington, DC: National Academy Press.

Brookfield, S. (1995) *Becoming a critically reflective teacher.* San Francisco, CA: Jossey Bass.

Brown, P., Lauder, H. and Ashton, D. (2008) *Education, globalisation and the knowledge economy: A commentary by the Teaching and Learning Research Programme.* Swindon, UK: Economic and Social Research Council.

Burroughs Wellcome Fund and Howard Hughes Medical Institute. (2006) *Making the right moves: A practical guide to scientific management for postdocs and new faculty* (2nd ed.). Available online at http://www.hhmi.org/labmanagement (accessed 25 November 2011).

Clarke, M. (2004) Reconceptualising mentoring: Reflections by an early career researcher. *Issues in Educational Research*, 14(2): 121–143.

Council Directive. (1999) *1999/70/EC*. Available online at http://eur-lex.europa.eu/LexUriServ/LexUriServ.do?uri=CELEX:31999L0070:EN:HTML (accessed 28 November 2011).

Crossouard, B. (2010) *Exploratory study of the early career trajectories of newly qualified researchers*. Helsinki, Finland: European Conference on Educational Research.

Davies, C. and Birbili, M. (2000) What do people need to know about writing in order to write in their jobs? *British Journal of Educational Studies*, 48(4), 429–445.

Davis, G. (2005) Doctors without orders. *American Scientist*, 93(3 Suppl.).

Day, A. (1996) *How to get research published in journals*. Aldershot, UK: Gower Press.

Delamont, S and Atkinson, P. (2004) *Successful research careers: A practical guide*. Maidenhead, UK: Open University Press.

Delamont, S., Atkinson, P. and Parry, O. (2004) *Supervising the PhD: A guide to success*. Maidenhead, UK: SRHE and Open University Press.

Dennett, D. C. (1991) *Consciousness explained*. London: Penguin.

Devine, E. B. (2009) The art of obtaining grants. *American Journal of Health-System Pharmacy*, 66(6): 580–587.

Economic and Social Research Council. (2005) *Research ethics framework*. Swindon, UK: ESRC. Available at: http://www.gold.ac.uk/media/ESRC_Re_Ethics_Frame_tcm6-11291.pdf (accessed 28 November 2011).

Economic and Social Research Council. (2010) *Framework for research ethics*. Swindon, UK: ESRC. Available at: http://esrcsocietytoday.ac.uk/_images/Framework_for_Research_Ethics_tcm8-4586.pdf (accessed 25 November 2011)

Elbow, P. (1973) *Writing without teachers*. Oxford, UK: Oxford University Press.

Eley, A. and Jennings, R. (2005) *Effective postgraduate supervision: Improving the student/supervisor relationship*. Maidenhead, UK: Open University Press.

Eley, A. and Murray, R. (2009) *How to be an effective supervisor: Best practice in research student supervision*. Maidenhead, UK: Open University Press.

European Commission. (2005) *European charter for researchers and the code of conduct for the recruitment of researchers*. Brussels: European Commission.

European University Association. (2007) *Doctoral programmes in Europe's universities: Achievements and challenges*. Brussels: European University Association.

Ferber, D. (1999) Postdoc activism: Irreconcilable differences. *Science*, 285(5433): 1516.

Fish, S. E. (2008) *Save the world on your own time*. New York: Oxford University Press.

Flint, K. (2010) *Responsible conduct of research toolkit: Tools for developing programs on responsible conduct of research for postdocs*. Washington, DC: National Postdoctoral Association.

Flower, L. and Hayes, J. (1981) The pregnant pause: An inquiry into the nature of planning. *Research in the Teaching of English*, 15(3): 229–243.

Fonseca-Kelly, Z., Operario, D. J., Finger, L. D., Jr., *et al.* (2010) The role of postdocs, PIs and institutions in training future scientists. *ASBMB Today*. Available at: http://www.asbmb.org/asbmbtoday/asbmbtoday_article.aspx?id=9198 (accessed 14 November 2011).

Garvey, R., Stokes, P. and Megginson, D. (2009) *Coaching and mentoring: Theory and practice.* London: Sage.

Glasersfeld, E. von (1995). *Radical constructivism: A way of knowing and learning.* Washington, DC: The Falmer Press.

Grabe, W. and Kaplan, R. (1996) *Theory and practice of writing.* New York: Longman.

Grove, L. K. (2004) Finding funding: Writing winning proposals for research funds. *Technical Communications*, 51(1): 25–35.

Harland, T. and Scaife, J. A. (2010) Academic apprenticeship. In T. Kerry (Ed.), *Meeting the challenges of change in postgraduate education* (pp. 179–180). London: Continuum

Hartley, J. (1992) Writing: A review of the research. In J. Hartley (Ed.), *Technology and writing: Readings in the psychology of written communication.* London: Jessica Kingsley.

Hartley, J. (1997) Writing the thesis. In N. Graves and V. Varma (Eds), *Working for a doctorate* (pp. 96–112). London: Routledge.

Hattie, J. (2009) *Visible learning: A synthesis of over 800 meta-analyses relating to achievement.* London: Routledge.

Hayes, J. and Flower, L. (1986) Writing research and the writer. *American Psychologist*, 41(10): 1106–1113.

Haynes, A. (2001) *Writing successful textbooks.* London: A and C Black.

Helbing, C. C., Verhoef, M. J., and Wellington, C. J. (1998) Finding identity and voice: A national survey of Canadian postdoctoral fellows. *Research Evaluation*, 7(1): 53–60.

Henson, K. (1999) *Writing for professional publication.* Boston, MA: Allyn and Bacon.

Higher Education Statistics Agency. (2011) *Statistics – Students and qualifiers at UK HE institutions.* Available at: http://www.hesa.ac.uk/index.php/content/view/1897/239 (accessed 25 November 2011).

James, L., Norman, J., De Baets, A., *et al.* (2009) *The lives and technologies of early career researchers.* Cambridge, UK: University of Cambridge. Available at: http://www.jisc.ac.uk/publications/reports/2009/earlycareerresearchersstudy.aspx

Johnson, A. M. (2009) *Charting a course for a successful research career: A guide for early career researchers.* Amsterdam: Elsevier.

Jones, R. (2003) Choosing a research question. *Asia Pacific Family Medicine*, 2(1): 42–44.

Keats, D. M. (2000) *Interviewing: A practical guide for students and professionals.* Buckingham, UK: Open University Press.

Klasen, N. and Clutterbuck, D. (2002) *Implementing mentoring schemes: A practical guide to successful programs.* Oxford, UK: Butterworth Heinemann.

Kreeger, K. (2003) A winning proposal. *Nature*, 426(6962): 102–103.

Lederman, D. (2007) Professional development for postdocs. *Inside Higher Ed.* Available at http://www.insidehighered.com/news/2007/08/20/postdoc (accessed 25 November 2011).

Lee, A., Dennis, C. and Campbell, P. (2007) Nature's guide for mentors. *Nature*, 447(7146): 791–797.

Lee, L. J., Gowers, I., Ellis, L., *et al.* (2010) Well-rounded postdoctoral researchers with initiative, who are not always 'tied to the bench' are more successful academically. *International Journal for Researcher Development*, 1(4): 269–289.

Lodge, D. (1988) *Nice work.* London: Secker and Warburg.

Loehle, C. (1990) A guide to increased creativity in research-inspiration or perspiration? *Bioscience*, 40(2): 123–129.

Marton, F. and Saljo, R. (1976) On qualitative differences in learning: I. Outcome and process. *British Journal of Educational Psychology*, 46(1): 4–11.

Mason, M. A. and Goulden, M. (2003) *Marriage and baby blues: Re-defining gender equality.* 'Fast Track': Success for Parents in Demanding Professions Conference, University of Pennsylvania, PA.

Medawar, P. (1963) Is the scientific paper a fraud? *The Listener*, September 1963.

Medawar, P. (1979) *Advice to a young scientist.* New York: Harper and Row.

Mervis, J. (1999) The world of postdocs [Introduction to the special issue]. *Science*, 285(5433): 1513.

Moxley, J. (1997) If not now, when? In J. Moxley and T. Taylor (Eds), *Writing and publishing for academic authors* (pp. 6–19). Lanham, MD: Rowman and Littlefield.

Murray, R. (2006) *How to write a thesis* (2nd ed.). Maidenhead, UK: Open University Press.

Murray, R. (2009) *How to survive your viva: Defending a thesis in an oral examination* (2nd ed.). Maidenhead, UK: Open University Press.

National Science Board. (2008) *Science and engineering indicators.* Arlington, VA: National Science Foundation.

Partridge, M. (2011) Careers for PhDs beyond academia. *Higher Education Guardian*, August 2011.

Phillips, E. M. and Pugh, D. S. (2010) *How to get a PhD: A handbook for students and their supervisors* (5th ed.). Maidenhead, UK: Open University Press.

QAA. (2004) *Code of practice for the assurance of academic quality and standards in higher education. Section 1: Postgraduate research programmes.* Available at: www.qaa.ac.uk/Publications/InformationAndGuidance/Documents/postgrad2004.pdf (25 November 2011).

Reich, E. S. (2011) Whistle-blower claims his accusations cost him his job. *Nature*, 474(7350): 140–141.

Reif-Lehrer, L. (2000) Applying for grant funds: There's help around the corner. *Trends in Cell Biology*, 10(11): 500–504.

Reis, R. M. (1999) Choosing a research topic. *The Chronicle of Higher Education.* Available online at http://chronicle.com/article/Choosing-a-Research-Topic/45641 (accessed 25 November 2011).

Reis, R. M. (2000) Choosing the right research adviser. *The Chronicle of Higher Education.* Available online at http://chronicle.com/article/Choosing-The-Right-Research/46388/ (accessed 25 November 2011).

Research Councils UK (2009) *RCUK policy and code of conduct on the governance of good research conduct: Integrity, clarity and good management.* Swindon, UK: Research Councils UK.

Research Councils UK. (2010) *Review of progress in implementing the recommendations of Sir Gareth Roberts, regarding employability and career development of PhD students and research staff.* Available at http://www.rcuk.ac.uk/documents/researchcareers/RobertReport2011.pdf (accessed 28 November 2011).

Richardson, L. (1990) *Writing strategies: Reaching diverse audiences.* Newbury Park, CA: Sage.

Richardson, L. (1998) Writing: A method of inquiry. In N. Denzin and Y. Lincoln (Eds), *Collecting and interpreting qualitative materials.* London: Sage.

Roberts, S. G. (2002) *SET for Success: The supply of people with science, technology, engineering and mathematical skills.* The Report of Sir Gareth Roberts' Review, Higher Education Funding Councils of England, Scotland and Wales. London: HM Treasury. Available at http://www.hm-treasury.gov.uk/documents/enterprise_and_productivity/research_and_enterprise/ent_res_roberts.cfm (accessed 25 November 2011).

Rousseau, A. and Eley, A. (2010) *Capturing best practice in postgraduate supervision: Taking a fresh look.* London: Society for Research into Higher Education.

Rugg, G. and Petre, M. (2010) *The unwritten rules of PhD research* (2nd ed.). Maidenhead, UK: Open University Press.

Scaife, J. A. (2007a) Lessons from a decade of constructivist initial teacher education in science. *Proceedings of the Second International Conference on Science and Mathematics Education*, November 2007, Penang, Malaysia, SEAMEO RECSAM (pp. 95–104).

Scaife, J. A. (2007b) Applications of constructivist initial teacher education in science: Addressing entrenched misconceptions in current electricity and light and colour. *Proceedings of the Second International Conference on Science and Mathematics Education*, November 2007, Penang, Malaysia, SEAMEO RECSAM (pp. 105–113).

Science. (1999) Postdocs working for respect [Special Issue]. *Science,* 285(5433): 1449–1628.

Second Annual Report on Research Staff, Funders Forum. (2009) Available at http://www.dti.gov.uk/policies/science/science-funding/funders-forum/reports (accessed 25 November 2011).

Sigma Xi Postdoc Survey. (2005) See data on Institutional Environment: http://postdoc.sigmaxi.org/ (accessed 28 November 2011).

Smedley, C. (1993) *Getting your book published.* Newbury Park, CA: Sage.

Steffe, L. and Gale, J. (1995) *Constructivism in education.* Hove, UK: Erlbaum.

Taylor, S. and Beasley, N. (2005) *A handbook for doctoral supervisors.* London: Routledge.

The National Academy of Sciences (2000) *Enhancing the postdoctoral experience for scientists and engineers: A guide for postdoctoral scholars, advisers, institutions, funding organisations and disciplinary societies* [Chapter 8, Principles, Action Points and Recommendations for Enhancing the Postdoctoral Experience]. Washington, DC: The National Academies Press.

The Scientist. (2006) A 10-step plan for better postdoc training: The research environment has evolved; it's time for the postdoctoral experience to do the same. *The Scientist,* 20(1): 24.

Thomas, G. (1987) The process of writing a scientific paper. In P. Hills (Ed.), *Publish or perish* (pp. 93–117). Ely, UK: Peter Francis.

Universities UK. (2005) *Research careers initiative.* Available at www.universitiesuk.ac.uk/activities/rci.asp (accessed 28 November 2011).

Universities UK. (2007) *Talent wars: The international market for academic staff* [Policy Briefing]. London, UK.

University and College Union. (2008) *The researcher's survival guide.* Available at www.ucu.org.uk/media/pdf/5/0/ucuressurvivalguide_apr08.pdf (accessed 28 November 2011).

Vitae. (2009a) *What do researchers do? First destination of doctoral graduates by subject.* Cambridge, UK: The Career Research and Advisory Centre (CRAC) Limited.

Vitae. (2009b) *What do researchers do? Career profiles of doctoral graduates.* Cambridge, UK: The Career Research and Advisory Centre (CRAC) Limited.

Vitae. (2009c) *Employers' briefing: Targeting the postgraduate and researcher market.* Vitae, AGCAS and AGR.

Vitae. (2010a) *What do researchers do? Doctoral graduate destinations and impact three years on.* Cambridge, UK: The Career Research and Advisory Centre (CRAC) Limited.

Vitae. (2010b) *Researcher development framework.* Available at http://vitae.ac.uk/researchers/1272-291181/Researcher-Development-Framework-RDF.html (accessed 28 November 2011).

Wason, P. C. (1980) Specific thoughts on the writing process. In L. Gregg and E. Steinberg (Ed.), *Cognitive processes in writing.* Hillsdale, NJ: Erlbaum.

Wellington, J. (2003) *Getting published.* London: Routledge.

Wellington, J. (2010) *Making supervision work for you: A student's guide.* London: Sage.

Wellington, J. and Szczerbinski, M. (2007) *Research methods for the social sciences.* London: Continuum.

Whitesides, G. (2004) Whitesides' group: writing a paper. *Advanced Materials,* 16(15): 1375–1377.

Wisker, G. (2005) *The good supervisor: Supervising postgraduate and undergraduate research for doctoral theses and dissertations.* Basingstoke, UK: Palgrave Macmillan.

Wolcott, H. (1990) *Writing up qualitative research.* Newbury Park, CA: Sage.

Woods, P. (1999) *Successful writing for qualitative researchers.* London: Routledge.

Woodwark, J. (1992) *How to run a paper mill: Writing technical papers and getting them published.* Winchester, UK: Information Geometers Ltd.

Wuchty, S., Jones, B. F. and Uzzi, B. (2007) The increasing dominance of teams in production of knowledge. *Science,* 316(5827): 1036–1039.

Yewdell, J. W. (2008) How to succeed in science: A concise guide for young biomedical scientists. Part 1: Taking the plunge. *Nature Reviews Molecular Cell Biology,* 9(5): 413–416.

Zinsser, W. (1983) *Writing with a word processor.* New York: Harper and Row.

Index